A Case Study: Motivating Disaffected Students Using Virtual Learning Environments to Raise Student Attainment

by Rashida Din

WORD COUNT 23844

CHARACTER COUNT 135920

TIME SUBMITTED 18-DEC-2012 03:14PM

PAPER ID 20468153

A Case Study: Motivating Disaffected Students Using Virtual Learning
Environments to Raise Student Attainment

Bedfordshire University

Master of Arts in the Faculty of Education,

January 2013

By

Rashida Din

1

Contents

Chapter 4: Methodology

Chapter 5: Presentation of Results

Abstract

Nationally research studies have explored how ICT can be used to motivate disaffected young people that are at risk of leaving school with little or no qualifications.   A local Pupil Referral Unit in a partnership approach with the Local Authority targeted students at a local Upper School at risk of being permanently excluded and leaving school with no national accreditation.

The Innovative use of VLE's was used as a vehicle to motivate students to complete accredited pathways in Literacy and Numeracy. Students identified they felt more motivated by using this approach. Furthermore key staff involved shared the student's views on the positive impact on motivation. All of the Year 11 students involved achieved at least one qualification in literacy or numeracy with an increased attendance at school. The literature review looked at the key research studies focusing on the impact of ICT on motivation. In addition how Learning Platforms could be used for virtual learning and collaborative opportunities for students was also explored. The key national political context agenda was the DCSF Children's Plan (2007) which focused on closing the gap in educational achievement for disadvantaged children.

Finally the study also identified that senior leaders had to be supportive of this type of intervention project and a whole school approach was necessary to embed this and drive future whole school improvement.

Acknowledgements

I would like to take this opportunity to thank my colleagues and friends for their patience and support. In particularly Akaash, Lorraine, Nasreen and Christine for their words of encouragement to complete this Masters research. Terry Ashmore Head teacher of the PRU for his support. And finally my dissertation supervisor Christina Kruegal for her constructive feedback. Thank you.

Chapter 1 : Introduction to the Study

1.1   Introduction

This study was set up to investigate if disaffected students can be motivated
to engage in learning to achieve nationally recognised qualifications. National
research studies have been conducted critically reviewing how ICT can
motivate young people. A key aim of the Department for Children, Schools
and Families' Children's Plan (DCSF 2007) is to close the gap in educational
achievement for disadvantaged children. These disaffected students are
target groups as they are at risk of being permanently excluded and
underachieve nationally in terms of progress and nationally recognised
accreditation.

Machin and McNally (2006), found strong evidence that education in
childhood improves future opportunities, for example, the likelihood of
employment and level of wages. It is of paramount importance that these
students are identified and intervention strategies put in place in mainstream
schools to ensure students achieve academically. In addition 'The Centre for
Research on the Wider Benefits of Learning' (DfES 2006b), found that, as well
as influencing the obvious outcomes i.e. qualifications and career, learning
can positively affect health and well-being, attitudes and behaviour.

A partnership approach with the Local Authority (LA), Pupil Referral Unit
(PRU) and a local school will be key. The local PRU has the statutory
responsibility for the education of all the LA pupils who have been
permanently excluded, or have long-term illness. Intervention projects with the
aim to reduce the numbers of students being permanently excluded also fall
within the remit of the PRU. Partnership working in schools is not a new
concept; however what is innovative is the use of Learning Platforms in
delivering academic content in personalised pathways leading to national
qualifications. The Department of Education (DoE), is responsible for

education and children's services nationally. At its heart is the National Agenda for Inclusion which details in practice the advantages of working in partnership with parents and agencies. This was to ensure schools offered educational provision that gave young people equal access and opportunities for successful learning (DoE, December 2011). These approaches are gaining an increasing influence in education and to quote Passey et al (2004: 3), *"consider the ways in which teachers could enhance motivational impacts for pupils, especially for those disaffected with traditional forms of learning"*. Could we consider a future where Virtual Learning Environments will in some instances replace a traditional classroom for students that are 'disaffected' and need a motivational tool based around the innovative use of ICT?

1.2   Aims

The aim of this research study will be to evaluate the use of innovative ICT and virtual learning to raise student motivation and attainment. The key objectives are:

- To identify the perceived motivational impact of ICT on students engagement to learning

- To evaluate student attainment and attendance whilst on this project

1.3   Research Questions

From the key objectives of this research study clear research questions can be formulated to give focus for this study. The key research questions are:

- What were the student perceptions on motivational levels when using virtual learning and was this supported by key staff involved with the project?
- What was the impact on student attainment and exam results?
- What was the impact on student's attendance whilst on the project taking into account school trends?

1.4   Statement of Purpose

The purpose of this research is to identify if ICT and virtual learning can raise student motivation in disaffected students and if so identify the impact on attainment, achievement and attendance.

1.5   Thesis Organisation

This research study is divided into seven chapters. The first chapter introduces and sets the national context of the research study and lays out the research studies objectives and key questions that will be answered.

The second chapter is the Part A of the literature review identifying the national trends in disadvantage and disaffection which affect young people. The link between motivation and the physiology human brain is discussed.. The third chapter is the Part B of the literature review. This section reviews national ICT studies linking student motivation and pedagogy. It also defines what a Learning Platform is and how current research studies are beginning to target the educational benefits. It then discusses the role of virtual learning and concludes with overview for the importance of staff ICT training.

The fourth chapter discusses the methodology used. This includes considering the research paradigm, method of research, data collection tools used and finally summarising the research ethics that where duly considered.

The fifth chapter presents the results from the student questionnaires, key staff interviews and looks at qualitative data such as student attainment and attendance.

The sixth chapter aims to analyse the results and seeks to answer the key objective and research questions on student and staff perceptions on motivation and student attainment and attendance. This will lead onto the recommendations, limitations of the study and further areas of research.

The final chapter will be the conclusion on successfully raising the motivation and attainment of disaffected young learners by the use of innovative ICT and virtual learning.

Chapter 2: The Literature Review Part A

2.1   Disaffection, Disadvantage and Attendance

Solomon and Rogers (2001) define disaffected students as those which are identified by staff as showing attributes such as disruptive behaviour in lessons, disruptive behaviour during lunch / break and other social times. In addition consistent breaking of school rules verbal abuse to staff and also drug abuse are indicators. In fact around one-third of children face some form of disadvantage which will impact on their educational attainment (Becta, 2007). It is key to understand the context of how disadvantage and disaffection can impact on each other. The factors which lead to disadvantage which Becta (2007), describe in great detail through the 'The Framework of Disadvantage' and the three tiers are summarised as the physical and socio-economic infrastructure, such as housing and schools. Relationships with family, friends and the local community, and the behavioural norms adopted through socialisation and finally identities developed through interpretation and internalisation of experiences (Becta, 2007).

In addition some of the key national trends for attainment are of interest for this research study. For example according to recent data from the Department of Enterprise, Trade and Investment 2006 (from the Office of National Statistics and DfES releases) state that most 19-year-olds without NVQ2 or its academic equivalent (for example, five or more good GCSEs) still lack such qualifications at age 25. Key also to note is that 25% of 19-year-olds still fail to achieve a basic level of qualification, and up to 10% have no qualifications at all and that 22% of pupils (150,000) aged 16 obtained no GCSEs above a grade D (DfES, 2006). And finally the authors note that3% of pupils (25,000) aged 16 achieved no GCSEs at all.

These trends are important as they highlight quite clearly that students that underachieve and have little or no qualifications will be at future disadvantage. What is worrying is that Becta (2007: 20) have also identified the following trends; that one in four 19-year-olds still fails to achieve a basic level of qualification, and up to one in ten has no qualifications at all. Furthermore the lower a young adult's qualifications; the more likely he or she is to be in low-paid work. So, for example, around half of employees aged 25–29 without any GCSEs at grade C or above are paid less than £6.50 per hour, compared with one in 10 of those with degrees or equivalent. In addition at age 16, over half of boys with poor reading skills think school is a waste of time, and nearly four-fifths want to leave school as soon as possible (National Literacy Trust 2005). The co-hort of students identified for this project as disaffected by the Upper School where mainly boys, which supports this statistic.

Furthermore truancy or non-attendance at school is a common feature of disaffected young people (Becta, 2007). Exclusion from school, as a sanction against a persistently disruptive pupil, can be permanent or fixed term. Excluded students in pupil referral units cost double the amount to be given one-10th of the education they could get in mainstream school, a point made by Parsons (996). Figures published by the Social Exclusion Unit (1998) indicates that 61% come from unemployed households, and young people in care are on average 10% more likely to be excluded than their peers.

Curriculum intervention projects which target disaffected groups and lead to the positive internalisation of attainment (Huitt, 2001), may go towards breaking the pathway and cycles of disadvantage. This gives further rationale to the project as students were identified by the partner school as those at risk of being permanently excluded and leaving with little or no qualifications.

2.2   Motivation and Brain Physiology

This next section aims to review scientific thinking in the field of psychology
focused on human motivation. There are numerous research studies on the
role of the brain and human motivation. Zull (2002) researched the
physiological structure of the brain in detail and what is of interest in this
research study was the link between the limbic cortex- the primitive area - of
the brain in controlling emotions and its negative influence. This primitive part
of the brain may result in anxiety which results in learners avoiding the work
and poor behaviour and thus reduced motivation. Huitt (2001), using Maslow's
'Hierarchy of Human Needs' interestingly also identify that student motivation
falls into two main groups namely intrinsic and extrinsic which Table 2.2.1
illustrates in more detail.

Intrinsic	Extrinsic
Explain or show why learning a particular content or skill is important	Provide clear expectations
Create and/or maintain curiosity	Give corrective feedback
Provide a variety of activities and sensory stimulations	Provide valuable rewards
Provide games and simulations	Make rewards
Set goals for learning	
Relate learning to student needs	
Help student develop plan of action	

**Table 2.2.1 – Intrinsic and extrinsic Motivation
(Source: Huitt, 2001:4)**

Furthermore Deci's (1975) work on the 'Self Determination Theory' is a field of psychology focused on human motivation and the extent where the degree to which behaviour is self motivated. In addition Deci focused on the idea of extrinsic versus intrinsic motivation, identifying intrinsically motivated learning as being undertaken for its inherent interest and enjoyment (Deci 1975). Passey et al (2004) highlighted and researched this link between ICT and intrinsic motivation. All of these factors are important for young learners to realise that they can achieve in terms of national qualifications if they can view it as personal success. Maslow (1987) identified that human behaviour is motivated by needs of self-determination or self-development; this forms the first principle of human behaviour and motivation.

2.3   Motivation and Teaching Strategies

Hattie (2009), has identified some examples of signposts towards excellence in education for example teachers are among the most powerful influences in learning. Furthermore teachers need to be directive, influential, caring and actively engaged in the passion of teaching and learning and in addition Teachers need to be aware of what each and every student is thinking and knowing, to construct meaning and meaningful experiences in the light of this knowledge, and have proficient knowledge and understanding of their content to provide meaningful and appropriate feedback (Hattie, 2009). Harlen and Crick (2003: 199) have identified that formal testing does not always have a motivating effect, especially for lower ability learners. They identify some teaching strategies to negate these include promoting learning goal (or mastery goal) orientation rather than performance goal orientation, cultivating intrinsic interest in the subject and putting less emphasis on grades but making grading criteria explicit. The authors are also list emphasising teaching approaches that encourage collaboration among students and cater for a range of teaching styles and finally explaining the reasons for, and the implications of tests.

Young (2005) identified the importance of self-regulated learning for his learners allowing them to fulfil their potential. Young (2005) identified a number of features of lessons that would enable more self-regulated learning which the VLE classroom and the use of Keyworkers will enable. This support includes giving positive feedback that supports development of competency, providing activity choice where possible and encouraging social connections in learning.

Sotto (1994) has suggested that teachers could help learning by enhancing what motivation learners entered the classroom with by the following classroom techniques involving learners in what they are being taught, where possible, making activities practical and collaborative, keeping learners actively engaged and finally pitching material at a suitable level for the learners.

Chapter 3 : Literature Review Part B

3.1   ICT Motivational Research Studies

Research literature for motivational patterns for students and the link to ICT
has greatly advanced over the last few years. The Department for Education
and Skills commissioned a study to investigate the motivational effect of
information and communication technologies and the outcomes where clear *"
schools led to positive motivational outcomes, supporting a focus upon
learning and the tackling of learning tasks"* (Passey et al, 2004:3). This
comprehensive ICT survey was across 17 schools and included interviews
with 121 teachers and 126 children. The report authors concluded that ICT in
schools motivates disaffected pupils and enabled pupils with special
educational needs to demonstrate the extent of their abilities (Passey et al,
2004).

The ICT in Schools Statistical Bulletins (DfEE, 2000; DfES, 2001; 2002; 2003)
indicate that levels of technology are increasing, such as the use of VLE,
hand held devices and data loggers across the curriculum. Further evidence
from the 'Fulfilling the Potential – Transforming Teaching and Learning
through ICT in Schools' (DfES, 2003) report illustrates how different forms of
technology can be applied to enhance-Learning and attainment and that
young people outside schools are accessing technology. The Gilbert Report
(DfES, 2006) expands on this and presents a vision for personalising teaching
and learning using innovative methods such as e-Learning (DfES, 2006).
Central to both of these reports was designing approaches for engaging and
raising the achievement of underachieving groups.

In addition there has also been an expectation from national government that
increased use of technology should enhance learning. This aim was set out in
its 2005 strategy paper 'Harnessing technology – transforming learning and

children's services'. That strategy is being implemented in a wide variety of ways and through various funding routes, with Becta being required to *"work with Government and its key agencies to create the conditions in the system that will lead to the majority of institutions and learning providers making more effective use of technology"* (OFSTED 2009:9). Furthermore one of the most influential papers for the benefits of ICT was Becta's report in 2008 'Meeting their potential: the role of education and technology in overcoming disadvantage and disaffection in young people'. To quote directly from this report 'Children *and young people are increasingly using ICT and the internet as a learning aid both in the classroom and for homework'* (Becta, 2008:68).

It is a worthy point to recognise that ICT tools students are familiar (Becta, 2008) and we as professionals need to capitalise on this. This understanding with pedagogy backed by an understanding of how ICT can personalise and enrich learning is key in raising achievement of disaffected young people. Dyer (2005) in his research discusses the new ICT pedagogies developing to encompass collaboration, and reflection. To develop this further Green et al (2005), states *''that the logic of education systems should be reversed so that it is the system that conforms to the learner, rather than the learner to the system''.* We have to be needs responsive - a key lesson to be learnt. This concept is known as personalising learning. Green et al, (2005) go on to say that *"personalisation demands a system capable of offering bespoke support for each individual that recognises and builds upon their diverse strengths, interests, abilities and needs in order to foster engaged and independent learners able to reach their full potential''.*

In October 2002, the Department for Education and Skills (DfES) commissioned a study to investigate the motivational effect of information and communication technologies (ICT) on pupils. This work was carried out by Passey et al (2004:16) and key findings admirably set the scene and context of this project study for example, ICT use by pupils and teachers in the case study schools led to positive motivational outcomes, supporting a focus upon learning and the tackling of learning tasks. In addition positive motivational outcomes were most frequently found when ICT was used to support engagement, research, writing and editing, and presentation of work. In addition boys and girls were both motivated by uses of ICT and the authors also concluded that there were indications that ICT impacted positively upon pupil behaviour inside school, and some impact on their behaviour outside school. Four theoretical models of motivation are discussed by Passey et al (2004), i.e. goals, interest, conceptions of ability; and intrinsic motivation. What is of interest is the authors exploration of motivational groups which can be broken down into 3 principle types and are part of this process of self-efficacy and long term change in motivation (Passey et al 2004:12). For example **learning goals**: engaging in the activity for personal understanding and competence; **performance approach goals**; engaging for positive feedback and finally **performance avoidance goals**: avoiding negative feedback. In addition Passey et al (2004:8) also define motivational measures and assign *"ideal positive learning profiles"* which are of interest for this study. Further definitions of motivational measure for this positive learning profile i.e. shown below in Table 3.1.1. In summary Passey et al (2004), key findings of their extensive studies on the motivational impact of learning highlighted that pupils and teachers in this sample of schools widely reported that using ICT has positive motivational impacts upon learning. The forms of motivation identified are supporting positive pupil commitment to a desire to learn and to undertake learning activities. In addition that a small number of teachers reported that motivation arising from the use of ICT is having an impact upon attainment.

Motivational measure	Definition	'Ideal positive' learning profile	'Ideal poor' learning profile
learning goal	the reason for engaging in the activity using ICT is the furtherance of personal understanding and competence	high level is desirable	low level is observed
academic efficacy	the degree to which an individual believes they have the capacity to design and execute the courses of action necessary to achieve a particular goal using ICT	high level is desirable	low level is observed
identified regulation	beginning to recognise and share the values that might have been assumed to drive the inducements offered by others to engage in the task using ICT	high level is desirable	low level is observed
intrinsic motivation	the degree to which ICT directly engages the pupil ands holds their interest	high level is desirable	low level is observed
performance approach goal	the reason for engaging in the activity using ICT is the pursuit of opportunities to gain positive feedback about one's competence	low level is desirable	high level is observed
performance avoidance goal	the aim of engaging in the activity using ICT is to avoid feedback suggestive of a lack of competence, often achieved by finding ways of not engaging in the task	low level is desirable	high level is observed
external regulation	A willingness to engage in work with ICT because one feels obliged to do so by someone else, probably an authority figure such as a teacher. One may recognise but not in anyway share the reasons why the other wants this	low level is desirable	high level is observed
amotivation	A lack of any particular reason for engaging with ICT supported work. There is no internal reason for wanting to engage in the work, and while others have told you that you must do it, it is not clear why	low level is desirable	high level is observed

Table 3.1.1 - 'Ideal' motivational profiles related to definitions of motivational measure (Passey et al, 2004:28)

Passey et al (2004) have identified eight motivational measures used in this study. Examples of classroom practices using ICT that do this are offered in Table 3.1.2:

Motivational measure	Implications for classroom practice	Examples of practice using ICT that enhance these measures
learning goals	an interest in learning and how to use techniques to learn should be enhanced by ensuring that process is considered as well as outcome	email is used to send a homework on presenting a summary of a poem to the teacher, the comments are used by the pupil to amend the work and to add to it, so that the successive drafts incorporate elements of an explicit ongoing process of subsequent learning
academic efficacy	knowing the techniques that can be used to learn should be enhanced	strategies used by individual pupils to tackle mathematical problems that are presented as starter exercises on the interactive whiteboard are picked up by the teacher and discussed with the class
intrinsic motivation	pupils should gain ownership of the learning activities they tackle	research using internet based or on-line resources is tailored to the individual by giving choice of topic to match pupil interests when possible
identified regulation	pupils should understand increasingly the reasons for engaging in learning activities	a graphics package is used to enable work to be created in the style of a specific artist, the teacher explores the reasons why this is useful, and how the work can be displayed on-line for others to view

Table 3.1.2: 'Ideal positive' motivational measures, their implications, and examples of classroom practice (Source: Passey et al, 2004: 71)

Examples of classroom practice using ICT that do this are given in Table 3.1.3

Motivational measure	Implications for classroom practice	Practice using ICT that limits this measure
performance approach goals	pupils should be encouraged to work together, to share and to compete against class targets as well as their own individual targets	mathematical starter activities are presented in quick succession on an interactive whiteboard, and pupils need to compete against the previous 'class' best mark
performance avoidance goals	pupils should be shown techniques that ICT can offer to enable work to be tackled	a pupil with writing difficulties is shown how a writing package enables writing to be changed easily, highlights words that can be checked, and how sentences and paragraphs can be moved around to shape a story for another reader
external regulation	pupils are encouraged to take enhanced ownership for learning activities	digital cameras are used to enable pupils to capture images during a visit, so that they can use these to recall events, and to write a story that relates to the things that they have chosen to capture as images
amotivation	pupils should become increasingly aware of why they are engaging in learning activities	the teacher wants pupils to create a scientific report on alternative energy sources, but discusses first the medium that pupils could use, in order to focus on the purpose of the report, how it will be used and by whom

Table 3.1.3 : 'Ideal poor' motivational measures, their implications, and examples of classroom practice (Source: Passey et al, 2004:71)

These features relate to the motivational measures and the relationship is illustrated in Table 3.1.4 below.

Feature	Relationship to motivational measures
equipment was deployed across the design and technology department	performance avoidance goal is reduced, while academic efficacy and intrinsic motivation are supported by deployment and access
computer access was available through desktop or laptop machines within workshops in each topic area	performance avoidance goal is reduced, while academic efficacy and intrinsic motivation are supported by deployment and access
each area within design and technology had subject specific software which was used, as well as generic software for word processing, presentation, and digital image capture and manipulation	learning goal and academic efficacy are supported by the software available, while performance avoidance goal is reduced
spreadsheets were used by staff to set targets, to monitor, and to track pupil performance, with pupils being aware of the process and seeking to maximise their attainment	learning goal and identified regulation are supported
word processing and desk top publishing software was used generally to produce draft and final versions of assignments	academic efficacy and learning goal are supported
presentational software was used by pupils and teachers to share and present ideas and summaries	academic efficacy, learning goal, intrinsic motivation and identified regulation are supported, while amotivation is reduced
email was used generally to send drafts to	academic efficacy, learning goal,

teachers for comment	intrinsic motivation and identified regulation are supported, while amotivation is reduced
digital cameras and digital image manipulation software were used in all areas from year 7 onwards	academic efficacy is supported
Key Stage 3 was divided into modules of work that was covered through separate design and technology areas, with all five areas being covered each year	intrinsic motivation is potentially supported
3D design packages were used routinely, to enable pupils to think from a 3D perspective, and to focus upon process and modelling rather than just upon task	academic efficacy, learning goal, intrinsic motivation and identified regulation are supported, while amotivation is reduced
CAD/CAM packages were used routinely to enable design to object to be seen easily	academic efficacy, learning goal, intrinsic motivation and identified regulation are supported, while amotivation is reduced
internet and CD-ROMs were used widely for research to match pupil needs and aspirations	intrinsic motivation and academic efficacy are supported
embroidery and sewing packages were used within the area of textiles for all pupils	academic efficacy, learning goal, intrinsic motivation and identified regulation are supported, while amotivation is reduced
subject specific software included electronic manipulation software, circuit design software, food analysis software and resistant material manipulation software	academic efficacy, learning goal, intrinsic motivation and identified regulation are supported, while amotivation is reduced
coursework templates for pupil assignments and as a basis for folders were created in word processing or desk	academic efficacy, learning goal, intrinsic motivation and identified regulation are supported, while

top publishing software, often with headers that highlighted the learning needs	amotivation is reduced
revision programs were used for certain topics	academic efficacy, learning goal, intrinsic motivation and identified regulation are supported, while amotivation is reduced

Table 3.1.4: Relationship of curriculum features to motivational measures (Source: Passey et al, 2004:28)

ICT is central to formal learning, with children and young people increasingly using ICT and the internet as learning aids both in the classroom and for homework (Condie and Munro 2007). Johnson and Dyer (2005) discuss the new ICT pedagogies developing to encompass collaboration, reflection and iteration. Futurelab (Green et al. 2005) states that 'the logic of education systems should be reversed so that it is the system that conforms to the learner, rather than the learner to the system'. This concept is known as personalising learning. Green et al. (2005) go on to say that *personalisation demands a system capable of offering bespoke support for each individual that recognises and builds upon their diverse strengths, interests, abilities and needs in order to foster engaged and independent learners able to reach their full potential'*. Becta (2007) also postulate that ICT can enable wider ranges of presentational styles and teaching approaches, satisfying different learning styles, eg widening use of interactive whiteboards and PDAs, and more generally sophisticated software and hardware. In addition online assessment and reporting tools which provide formative as well as summative feedback for pupils and teachers, the development of higher-order skills; for example, analysis and synthesis through independent and collaborative research. Finally the broadening of options through e-learning provision; in addition, virtual learning environments can give learners more control of their own learning pathways and preferences with any time, anywhere learning (Becta, 2007).

3.2   Motivation and Collaborative ICT

To start with we need to recognise why collaborative e-Learning is seen to be
a successful way to learn. Hiltz (1998) achieved this by looking at practical
examples and theoretical approaches and identified that the potential negative
effects of online courses which is a loss of social relationships and of the
sense of community. Furthermore Huitt (2001) concluded that to achieve
collaborative learning strategies, a requirement was relatively small classes or
groups actively mentored by an instructor. In addition Huitt (2001) also
identified the importance of motivation and defines how emotions can affect
this. Both extrinsic and intrinsic motivation is broken down. In fact Laister et
al, (2002) identified that innovative Learning Platforms need to be built on
collaborative social learning.

Vygotskys (1978) in his influential research observed children can develop
higher mental functions through social interactions in a process of
internalisation. In addition language can play a central role in mental
development. Furthermore collaboration is viewed as the process of building
and maintaining a shared understanding of a problem (Laister et al, 2001). In
this context virtual collaborative e-Learning is when these interactions take
place in virtual environments.

McNamee and Roberts (2010), highlight clearly the benefit of learner centred
learning 'The use of collaborative learning implies a change from teacher-
centred learning to a focus on learner-centred learning, with knowledge
acquisition being assisted by student interaction, evaluation and cooperation'.
Furthermore they identify examples of collaborative learning activities
(McNamee and Roberts, 2010) for example group projects, simulation and
role-playing exercises, collaborative composition of essays, debates and
finally seminar-style presentations and discussions. (Hiltz & Turoff, 1993, cited
in Hiltz, 1998).

Laister and Kobek (2001), define collaborative learning as *"any kind of group learning in which there are some meaningful learning interactions between learners ....virtual collaborative e-learning if these interactions take place in virtual environments"*. Hilz (1998) highlights evidence that collaborative learning strategies, which require relatively small classes or groups actively mentored by an instructor, are necessary in order for Web-based courses to be as effective as traditional classroom courses. In addition Webb (1984) also identify the interaction and learning in small group and whole-class settings and conclude that students are better motivated in small group settings. Taking this into account the students groups we have set up are no more than four in size.

Further work by Laister et al, (2001), identified that past and some present e-Learning technologies are mainly resource based with the mayor focus on the interaction between human and computers. The main disadvantage identified again by the authors is the lack of peer contact and interaction, high initial costs for preparing multimedia content and for maintaining and updating this content as well as the need for flexible tutorial support. These findings are relevant especially since collaborative learning is seen as a successful way to learn. It is the learning theory which supports this which is of interest in the research study. In addition Laister and Kobek, (2001:3) using Piagets and Vgostoskys theories have identified the importance of the relevance of knowledge to the learner in order to achieve long term effective learning as *'the concept of the learner as constructing his own world of content, as he confronts newly-learned material with his existing knowledge'*. Vgostokys, (1978) theory is based upon the interaction of people and virtual collaborative e-Learning opportunities will be created where students as peers will work and understand each other to learn with the four main points summarised as children construct their own knowledge, development can not be separated from its social context. In addition earning can lead to development and finally language can play a central role in mental development

In addition Hilz (1998:1), states clearly that passive approaches to learning assume that students "learn" by *'receiving and assimilating knowledge individually .... In contrast, active approaches present learning as a social process which takes place through communication with others'*. With this in mind the VLE has been set up to be collaborative for students, peer mentors and the school based Keyworker. Online forum rooms have been created with students and staff having access to the resources and threads. Hilz (1998) highlights this as good practice 'Every "electure" (electronic lecture) should be designed to include questions for discussion or response among groups of students, rather than simply representing one way transmission of "knowledge." The students, as well as the instructor, should be encouraged to raise new topics and ask questions of the class; and to respond to one another's contributions'. On the empirical data side Laister and Kobek (2001), go on to highlight that empirical research shows that collaborative learning compared to individual and competitive learning scenarios brings students to a higher achievement level, raises their problem solving- abilities, offers cognitive advantages to learners and also has positive influences in enhancing the development of personality traits that are beneficial for future learning.

There are strengths of collaborative learning which McNamee and Roberts (2001) discuss this more thoroughly. Limitations include students need to be familiar with software, hardware and its uses or problems that may arise. *'When accessing a live chat session, an email discussion group or a workspace session, an unskilled student may become frustrated and the collaboration process may become obstructed' conclude McNamee and Roberts* (2001:4). What is critical to this research study are the good practice 'tips' or guidelines identified by the authors the that would benefit students with regard to the technology used (Agostinho, Lefore and Hedberg (1997)) that training to use the technology is essential. In addition this can be supplied outside of normal lecture times or as part of the first meeting and it should be in clear non-technical language, which facilitates the students' use of the tools and explains clearly what technical equipment is required from the students for the course (McNamee et al, 2001). The authors also conclude that a support person should be accessible by the students out of hours so all technical problems are dealt with quickly thus ensuring students do not become over frustrated with the technology and that the initial weeks of the course should involve small collaboration or discussion projects, which involve students in using the tools from the outset – before they are required for assessable tasks.

3.3 Learning Platforms

This section will aim to look at how a LP be used for virtual learning
opportunities. Becta was the government agency which led the national drive
to ensure the effective and innovative use of technology throughout learning
and the use of LP. Becta (2006) acknowledged that a learning platform is not
expected to be a single product but rather a collection of interoperable
systems or modules from different suppliers. Each may perform discrete
functions, but collectively they should deliver the requirements. Basically it
provided the infrastructure to where virtual resources can sit and be used in
the form of Virtual Learning Environments (VLE). These requirements are
listed below (Becta, 2006:5-11) and are further elaborated in Appendix 1:

- Content management – enabling teaching staff to create, store and
  repurpose resources and coursework which can be accessed online
  (Table 3.3.1)
- Curriculum mapping and planning – providing tools and storage to
  support assessment for learning, personalisation, lesson planning etc.
  (Table 3.3.2)
- Learner engagement and administration –enabling access to pupil
  information, attendance, timetabling, e-portfolios and management
  information (Table 3.3.3)
- Tools and services – providing communication tools such as email,
  messaging, discussion forums and blogs (Table 3.3.4)

Table 3.3.1 - Content management

Requirement name	Description	Notes
R1: Assessment items	Assessment items shall be loaded and used.	Platforms shall be able to deal with assessment items including those meeting selected open specifications that define question types and how they can be delivered.
R2: Launch resources	The user shall be able to launch digital content via a web browser or other application.	Specified World Wide Web Consortium (W3C) specifications shall be supported, including being able to use the hypertext transfer protocol (http) and the hypertext markup language (html). The appropriate e-Government Interoperability Framework requirements shall be met. Filtering systems that block the receipt of inappropriate materials and access to undesirable websites should be enabled but this is largely the responsibility of the ISP.

Requirement name	Description	Notes
R3: Load content objects	It shall be possible to load, store and make sharable content objects available to users. Run-time interactions with content objects should be supported. This includes being able to load bundled resources (content packages) and unpack them.	Parts of the SCORM specification shall need to be supported.
R4: Load resources	It shall be possible to load digital content into a storage area that can be presented to learners and accessed via the platform interface.	The appropriate file type requirements in the e-Government Interoperability Framework shall be met.
R5: Metadata creation	Users shall be able to classify and tag resources.	If metadata is to be shared a profile of the Curriculum Online format shall be used. It is recognised that in order to keep tagging simple not all elements will be needed. Other metadata schemes may be used. It should be possible for local information to be recorded and used and for metadata to be created socially (for example, folksonomy).

Requirement name	Description	Notes
R6: Metadata import and display	It shall be possible to load and store metadata records and display information derived from them to the user.	There are various possible metadata formats including Curriculum Online and e-Government Metadata Standards (eGMS). It is recognised that there may be a range of metadata provided and it may not be possible to provide consistent information.
R7: Resource creation	Users shall be able to create new resources, integrate them with the platform and export them.	It is important that learner can be engaged with digital tools as well as have access to ready-made content. This could include collaborative resource creation, bookmarking and creation of annotations or ratings.
R8: Coursework	Schools should be able to submit pupils' coursework (formally agreed and accredited units of study) to examination bodies in an agreed format.	There is no currently agreed specification although some formats have been produced for specific cases. This is also dependent on other issues such as non-repudiation and security. Consideration should also be given to submission of coursework to colleges or for use in a portfolio.
R9: Cross device	Resources should be made available to a range of devices.	There is increasing use of various devices to support learning. These will be determined by the context but could include mobile devices such as PDAs and cell phones.

Requirement name	Description	Notes
R10: Identifiers	Globally unique identification namespaces should be interpreted and managed.	Identification of resources and individuals should be unambiguous. The platform should support the W3C Uniform Resource Identifier (URI) format and specified coding schemes such as the Unique Pupil Number.
R11: Resource lists	Lists of resources should be made available in a shareable format.	Reading lists could be exchanged or shared both within and across schools, and with other users and the community.
R12: Syndicate content	Users should be able to combine data-streams and selectively share them with others.	Data could be gathered from personal or class-based web logs, news sites and subject-based blogs, podcasts, vodcasts or newsfeeds and sites and distributed as 'remixes' or 'playlists'.

(Source: Becta, 2006:5)

Table 3.3.2 - Curriculum mapping and planning

Requirement name	Description	Notes
R13: Accessibility	The platform interface shall be accessible to users.	It is the responsibility of a platform provider to ensure accessibility guidelines are followed and that legislation such as the Disability Discrimination Act is adhered to. A detailed set of guidelines for accessibility is not considered to be within the scope of this framework and full Web Accessibility Initiative (WAI) AAA requirements may be too restrictive. Requirements for learners and administrators may vary. It is recognised that the platform provider may not have control over the accessibility of content. However, WAI AA level requirements should be met by platform modules.
R14: Assessment for learning	The platform shall enable learners to be provided with assessments and diagnostics to support learning plans.	This should include self-review and peer review.

Requirement name	Description	Notes
R15: Customisable interface	The user interface shall be capable of being customised to adapt to the learner's preferences.	This should include learner interface preferences and accessibility requirements. The user shall be able to change the screen colours, font and font size.
R16: Lesson planning	It shall be possible for teachers to produce and manage lesson plans.	HTML or other open formats should be used. A lesson plan specification could be developed in collaboration with all the major stakeholders and it could then be possible to share plans more widely.
R17: Navigation and search	Curriculum information shall be used to search for and to navigate to resources within the platform.	A recognised curriculum format shall be used. In particular specified Curriculum Online structures shall be used. Metadata and Topic Maps offer possible ways to express these structures.
R18: Personalisation	Users should be able to personalise their learning experience.	This should include using a learner profile to adjust the resources that are presented. The platform should also allow the learner to select aspects of their own learning journey.

(Source: Becta, 2006:7)

Table 3.3.3 - Learner engagement and administration

Requirement name	Description	Notes
R21: Access off site	Users shall be able to access the learning platform away from the organisation.	The intention is to enable anytime anywhere access and to include all types of users including teachers, pupils and parents. It is recognised, however, that this depends on access to an appropriate infrastructure and upon the license conditions for some published resources.
R22: Authentication	Users shall be uniquely identified and verified.	There should be a consistent approach to authentication; for example, every user may have a unique user name and password linked to individual or group roles and privileges and can easily access other systems. Common systems, including Shibboleth, should be used. Providers should take steps to avoid unauthorised access.

Requirement name	Description	Notes
R23: Consistent learner information	Learner information shall be consistent throughout the platform	There should be minimal duplication of information and processes should be automated to avoid errors and inconsistencies. A hub integration model could be adopted that allows data to be shared and managed across several systems. Learner information could alternatively only be accessed through a single shared service.
R24: Data protection	All stored data shall be secure.	Conformance with current legislation and the requirements of the Data Protection Act for personal data shall be required.
R25: Groups and roles	It shall be possible for users be allocated to one or more groups and assigned roles.	Roles and permissions affect how users can interact with the platform. Roles include, for example, administrator, teacher, parent or pupil.
R26: Information access	Users with privileges shall be able to access appropriate information.	This could include management information exchanged transparently between systems that may be outside the platform. This could also include support for selective disclosure by electing to share information or resources with other users.

Requirement name	Description	Notes
R27: Learner information export	It shall be possible for learner information to be exported from the platform.	This shall include support for the provision of statutory information to the DfES or other authorities.
R28: Learner information Import	It shall be possible for learner information to be imported to the platform.	This shall include support for transfer of learner records between institutions.
R29: Portfolios	Users shall be able to create and maintain portfolios for sharing content and to support personal development.	This kind of functionality is sometimes provided as part of an e-portfolio. But 'e-portfolio' has various definitions and there are several functions that can be provided, possibly via links to a range of web services. Portfolios could include goal setting, identifying interests and learning plans. It is expected that there will be further work to help clarify e-portfolio functionality.
R30: Scheduling	Access to resources shall be controllable.	Access may depend upon time constraints or be linked to other events. For example, access to a task may be dependent upon successful completion of another task or only be available for a set time linked to a timetable.

Requirement name	Description	Notes
R31: Tracking	Facilities shall be provided to track learners' support needs and performance.	This shall include reporting whether a learner has completed a particular resource or could include more complex scores or assessment data. Tracking information should be used to provide feedback to learners.
R32: Usage data	Information about individual and group usage of the resources shall be available.	Reports shall be generated that summarise how and when the platform and resources are used.
R33: Attendance	Support should be provided for the measurement and reporting of attendance.	For example by providing interfaces to support attendance recording by teachers, or integration with automated attendance or tracking devices.
R34: Self-organisation	Users should be able to organise and annotate resources.	This should include categorising and making connections, bookmarking, playlists, adding their own comments, tags and ratings. These could be shared with others.
R35: Timetabling	A timetable, or an interface to one, should be supported.	This could be linked to a personalised learning space and scheduling of resources.

(Source: Becta, 2006:9)

Table 3.3.4 - Table 4 Tools and services

Requirement name	Description	Notes
R36: Discussion forums	Users shall be able to take part in discussion forums by posting and reading messages.	Both intranet and internet services could be considered and desktop clients as well as web clients. Forums should be manageable, for example, for a particular group for a set period.
R38: Web services	The platform shall be capable of transparently interacting with web services using standard protocols.	This requirement does not at this stage specify particular services, just that there is capability to meet web services protocols when they are required. For example, users could search the Curriculum Online portal from within the platform if this functionality is made available.
R39: Audio-visual conferencing	Audio- and video-conferencing should be supported.	This should enable voice or visual communication with peers or teachers, for example using voice over internet protocol (VOIP).
R40: Blog	Users should be able to create web logs.	This could include a facility for multimedia entries and integration of an e-portfolio with selective disclosure.

Requirement name	Description	Notes
R41: Email	One-one and one-many messaging should be facilitated.	Email, or a system that is like email, should be available to users for sending and receiving. This should include sending messages to lists of recipients. Though this is likely to be the responsibility of the ISP, a platform should be able to integrate with email.
R42: Knowledge construction	Knowledge construction tools should be available.	These should include collaborative tools, such as Wikis, that allow for the shared editing of content. The tools may be within or outside the platform.
R43: Messaging	Users should be able to send messages to individuals and groups of users.	Sending SMS text messages to mobile phones should be supported. The messages could be multimedia as well as text.
R44: Other activities	Support for non-teaching activities should be provided.	Tools for managing teaching activities should be flexible and usable for non-teaching activities, created and managed both by teachers and pupils as appropriate. Activities could include sports teams, clubs and societies, community action and student projects.

(Source: Becta, 2006:11)

3.4   Virtual Learning Environments

OFSTED (2008) defined Virtual Learning Environments (VLE's) as computers that allow remote access to learning however this has developed and key points defined by on OFSTED (2009:8) *'where a VLE is a computer-based system that helps learning'.* Many terms and systems are associated with VLE's. One used routinely is managed learning environment (OFSTED, 2008). This usually describes the infrastructure needed to deliver the VLE, and may include other aspects linked with learning, such as attendance records, reports or room allocation. The combination of a VLE and managed learning environment is sometimes known as a Learning Platform (OFSTED, 2008).

In addition OFSTED (2006), identified that the best VLE's enhanced learning, giving learners the opportunity to reinforce aspects of their work as well as the chance to catch up on missed material. VLE's were least effective when they had little content or were just a dumping ground for rarely used files. The main factor behind a successful VLE area was the enthusiasm of individual teachers or trainers and often linked with their good use of technology to improve learning in the classroom or workshop. The best VLE's also had strong support from senior managers with good resources for development and maintenance. However in their research studies only three institutions had VLE strategies and none of the institutions had comprehensive formal quality assurance arrangements for VLE material to confirm accuracy, relevance, currency, suitability, or usage (OFSTED, 2006).

There was no correlation between effective VLE's and any particular subject area. The main factor behind a successful VLE area was the enthusiasm of individual teachers or trainers and often linked with their good use of technology to improve learning in the classroom or workshop. The authors also concluded that the best VLE's had strong support from senior managers with good resources for development and maintenance. However the self-assessment of VLE's and their impact on learning was underdeveloped.

Furthermore direct costs associated with introducing and running a VLE were not a particular concern for larger organisations and those using systems freely available on the internet.

3.5   Virtual Classrooms

Galloway et al (2001) are keen to show that current educational virtual environments are large and extensive and can be difficult to define as they are constantly changing and evolving, and are keen to divide these into three broad categories. The first is that independent models can often be referred to as "asynchronous" because they do not rely upon direct communication between teachers and students, as they do not avail of chat or videoconferencing facilities. Students access and interact with materials at their convenience and so the learning structure is considered unscheduled. Secondly synchronous models usually involve more communication and collaboration through videoconferencing and live chats so there are more opportunities for socializing (Galloway et al, 2001). As online meetings are usually scheduled there is limited flexibility. These are typical features of online-Learning as illustrated by Preece, (2000) in Table 3.5.1 :

Synchronous Tools	Asynchronous Tools
• Audio Conferencing	• Discussion Boards
• Web Conferencing	• Calendar
• Video Conferencing (live link)	• Website Links
• Chat	• Group Announcements
• Instant Messaging	• Messaging / E-mail
• White Boarding	• Surveys & Polls
	• Decision Support Tools

Content Integration	Document Management
• Interactive CBTs	• Resource Library
• Streaming Audio & Video	• Document Collaboration
• Narrated Slideshows	• Version Tracking & Control
• Web books	• Permission Based 2Access

Table 3.5.1

Synchronous and Asynchrous Learning examples

(Source: Preece, 2000:1)

While recognising little research has been done to demonstrate the effect on
student performance within virtual classrooms and traditional classrooms
Furthermore Galloway et al (2001:1) do conclude from their research literature
that *'that the traditional classroom could be sometimes an inhibiting
environment for students, and its structure can be pressurising and intimating.
Whereas the virtual environment encourages freedom of expression and
students are more open to communicate and express opinion and would often*

thrive in these environments'. Further evidence from their literature research concludes the virtual students seemed more frustrated not from only the technology but from the inability to, ask the teacher, questions in a face-to-face environment (Galloway et al, 2001). Or simply put many different strategies need to be used to have a blended learning experience for the students taking into account different learning styles. This research study seeks to do this as there will be 1:1 lessons supplementing the work online, with a dedicated Keyworkers available in the school.

3.6   Virtual Versus Traditional Classroom

While recognising little research has been done to demonstrate the effect on student performance within virtual classrooms and traditional classrooms Galloway et al (2001:2) conclude from their research literature that *'that the traditional classroom could be sometimes an inhibiting environment for students, and its structure can be pressurising and intimating'*. Whereas the virtual environment encourages freedom of expression and students are more open to communicate and express opinion and would often thrive in these environments'. Further evidence from their literature research concludes *'the virtual students seemed more frustrated', not from only the technology but from the inability to, ask the teacher, questions in a face-to-face environment'* (Galloway et al, 2001:2). The authors also argue only when learning environments, and those involved are fully responsive to the needs of students will optimal levels of progress take place. Or put it simply many different strategies need to be used to have a blended learning experience for the students taking into account different learning styles.

3.7   ICT Training Requirements

This section will look at how to identity ICT training needs of staff to use a LP. One of the key elements was the training of staff as there is variation in the use and skill levels of teaching staff using ICT. The Becta Harnessing Technology survey (Kitchen et al, 2007) reported that digital resources are used on average for 43% of primary teachers' lesson planning and 34% of secondary teachers' lesson planning and in addition the majority of teachers (58% of primary and 65% of secondary teachers) create their own digital learning resources. ICT is mostly used for whole-class activities. Two-fifths (41%) of secondary teachers made use of subject-specific software applications in at least half of lessons (Becta, 2007).

In addition Selwyn (1997), found that a major deterrent to the use of computers by teachers was computer phobia caused by psychological factors such as having little or no control over the activity, thinking that they might damage the computer, and feeling that one's self esteem is threatened. Also sociological factors such as ICT being regarded as a solitary activity, needing to be clever to use one, and being replaced by the computer and finally operational factors such as being beyond one's abilities, having to cope with unfriendly jargon, and the likelihood of the technology going wrong.

3.8   Case study 1 (Source: OFSTED, 2006)

Adaptation of an integrated learning technology practitioners programme to develop individual competence in using a VLE to support learning

Background

The Integrated Learning Technology Practitioners Program is a Havering College staff development course which is designed to provide staff with the practical skills required to make full use of the e-learning resources available to them at the college. It has been adapted from the FERL integrated learning technology programme and now has a focus on achieving key aspects of competence to meet the college's strategic expectations and goals for e-learning. The units of the course include the use of the SMART Board and the SMART Notebook. Also the use of the Blackboard virtual learning environment at Level 1 (basic) and Level 2 (advanced) and finally simple ways of introducing interactivity to course materials (OFSTED, 2006).

Delivery methods

The delivery method can be face to face, online, or a blend of the two. All course material is available on the college VLE. Assessment is by online submission of and the course is intended to take a total of 30 hours to complete, including tutorials and assignment work (OFSTED, 2006).

Award

Successful completion of the course leads to a nationally recognised level 2 award in information technology, validated by the awarding body Aberdeen Skills and Enterprise Training (OFSTED, 2006).

3.9   Case study 2:

Collaborative working to introduce and exploit a VLE (Source: OFSTED, 2006)

Introduction and background

The National Institute for Adult and Continuing Education (NIACE) funded the TeesLearn VLE development, using Moodle as its platform. The adult education services of five local authorities originally shared the development and maintenance of the VLE: Redcar and Cleveland; Darlington; Hartlepool; Stockton-on-Tees; and Middlesbrough. County Durham recently joined the partnership (OFSTED, 2006).

The partnership

The Tees Valley local authorities have a long-established history of collaborative work. When NIACE initially requested bids for Moodle development, individual bids could not exceed £20,000. They estimated that, as individual local authorities in a relatively small area, there was little chance that all would have successful bids. Instead, one local authority, Stockton-on-Tees, led the successful bid for the whole of the partnership – £50,000 – which was used to fund the TeesLearn development (OFSTED, 2006).

Chapter 4: Methodology

4.1   Introduction

Research has its origins and motivation in the researcher's curiosity and desire and seeks conclusions with evaluations lead to decisions (Cohen et al, 2011). There are three broad approaches to education research which Cohen et al (2003) refers to in great detail. The first is the scientific paradigm that can be tested, the second approach is to understand and interpret the world and the third is the political and ideological approach. This research study has used the second approach primarily as case studies can establish cause and effect in a real context (Cohen et al, 2003). This chapter will outline the research paradigm, leading onto the method of research and the data collection methods employed. Research ethics, limitations, reliability, validity and triangulation will conclude this chapter.

4.2   The Research Paradigm

The research paradigm refers to the deductive/inductive and qualitative/quantitative approaches employed. Marcoulides (1998) clearly defines the deductive approach as a testing of theories however the inductive approach, on the other hand, follows from the collected empirical data and forms concepts and theories on the basis of this data.

This is essentially a top down or bottom up approach illustrated by Trochim, (2001). This research study follows the deductive approach primarily as it is the most scientific but will oscillate towards the inductive approach when needed. As Cresswell (2003), states the research approach influences design and may contribute to or limit this study. To develop this further Burton et al, (2008), also examines in detail two of the main models of educational research which are positivistic/scientific (experimental) and interpretative. Interpretative research can lead to a deeper understanding or insight by collecting mainly qualitative data, which indicate possible routes for improvement.

The positivistic approach will also factor as it seeks hard quantitative data with research producing policies and this approach will be used in the main and enhanced with qualitative data collection (Burton et al, 2008). In addition Ryan (2006) also explores the positivist approach. This has a role as quantitative research has positivist features when it tries to link variables, test theories or hypotheses and finally tries to isolate and define categories before research starts and then to determine the relationships between them.

The philosophical basis is a subjectivist one where idealism features as the world exists but different people construe it in different ways. The interpretive paradigm carried out by gathering predominantly qualitative data to gain a deeper understanding of phenomena examined through actions and behaviour and can only enhance this study.

4.3   The Qualitative vs the Quantitative Approach

Ryan (2006), seeks to qualify the role of qualitative data further as it seeks to provide an in-depth picture and values participants' perspectives on their worlds. The qualitative approach strengths will mean the individuals interpretation of events will be important and thus will be 'rich'.

Quantitative data is more efficient and able to test hypotheses Neill (2007), highlights the advantages and disadvantages of using one approach over the other, and taking this into account this blended approach will seek to provide a balance (Table 1).

The quantitative tools for data analysis generally borrow from the physical sciences, in that they are structured in such a way so as to guarantee (as far as possible), objectivity, and reliability (Creswell, 2003). This research will use both methods as tools for data collection and analysis. Neill (2007) breakdowns the features of qualitative and quantitative research in Table 4.3.1 below in much more detail.

Qualitative	Quantitative
"All research ultimately has a qualitative grounding" - Donald Campbell	"There's no such thing as qualitative data. Everything is either 1 or 0" - Fred Kerlinger
The aim is a complete, detailed description.	The aim is to classify features, count them, and construct statistical models in an attempt to explain what is observed.
Researcher may only know roughly in advance what he/she is looking for.	Researcher knows clearly in advance what he/she is looking for.
Recommended during earlier phases of research projects.	Recommended during latter phases of research projects.
The design emerges as the study unfolds.	All aspects of the study are carefully designed before data is collected.
Researcher is the data gathering instrument.	Researcher uses tools, such as questionnaires or equipment to collect numerical data.
Data is in the form of words, pictures or objects.	Data is in the form of numbers and statistics.
Subjective - individuals' interpretation of events is important ,e.g., uses participant observation, in-depth interviews etc.	Objective – seeks precise measurement & analysis of target concepts, e.g., uses surveys, questionnaires etc.
Qualitative data is more 'rich', time consuming, and less able to be generalized.	Quantitative data is more efficient, able to test hypotheses, but may miss contextual detail.
Researcher tends to become subjectively immersed in the subject matter.	Researcher tends to remain objectively separated from the subject matter.

Table 4.3.1 - Features of Qualitative & Quantitative Research (Source: Neill, 2007:1)

4.4   The Instrument: The Case Study

A case study is a deep and detailed examination of a context (Burton et al, 2008) a study into the *'cause and effect'*. The case study research sits within the vision and principles of the LA (LA, 2008:1) especially as it will *" be owned by the school, be collaborative and importantly embrace national, regional and school ICT requirements"*.

The Upper School was approached by the LA and the PRU with the proposal. Disaffection is term which Solomon and Rogers (2001), highlight as a umbrella term to 'describe a variety of problematic behaviours and attitudes'. The pastoral Deputy Head at the Upper School in conjunction with the PRU initially identified twenty disaffected Key stage 4 students and using the criteria for disaffection set out by Solomon and Rogers (2001). This criteria included disruptive behaviour in lessons, during lunch / break and other social times. Other attributes include breaking of school rules verbal abuse to staff and drug abuse. In addition the students where all also considered to be at risk of leaving school with little or no qualifications. As Kothari (2005:15) states a judgement sampling process can *'secure reactions to a new way of teaching'*. However by the time the project was underway at the start of the spring term, one student had been permanently excluded and four students did not want to take part in the project. The students that where chosen to be part of the project study where aged between 14-16 years and the final cohort consisted of ten year 10 students and five year 11 students. One student was permanently excluded early on in the project and allocated another school.

The Upper School has been a specialist college since 2002. The majority of students are from White British backgrounds with a high proportion eligible for free school meals. The proportion of students in receipt of additional support due to their learning difficulties and or disabilities is also higher than average. The school is subject to consultation on closure with an aim to open an

Academy in September 2009. The school now provides a satisfactory education for its students and satisfactory value for money: good progress has been made since November 2006 and there is good capacity to build on the improvements (OFSTED Report October 2008). In 2010 the school retained 'Notice to Improve' status from OFSTED.

The e-Learning project is blended learning which is best defined as *'learning communities which integrate online learning and face-to-face meetings' (Kaplan, 2006:1)*. There are two core assumptions that underlie approaches to building blended learning communities: (1) that the deeper the personal relationships between learners, the richer the collaborative learning experience; and (2) that relationships between learners may be strengthened through structuring group interactions (using technology) before and/or after an face-to-face training event' (Kaplan, 2006). Students will have the benefit of both online resources and face to face lessons with the Key worker and student peer mentor. The author also frameworks the model in practice will incorporate the following elements. For example **'Clearly Defined Roles'** - Relationship between the different roles in the community (i.e. students, e-Learning Key worker, **'Creating Sub-Groups'** - sub-groupings of learners that have their own online space for small group learning activities and group project collaboration and finally **'Support Individuality'** - Provide a way for learners to create personal profiles that contain their photos and salient information to the topic at hand.

4.4.1 Case Study: Virtual Classroom

The VLE has been set up to be collaborative for students, peer mentors and the school based Keyworker. Online forum rooms have been created with students and staff having access to the resources and threads. Hilz (1998) highlights this as good practice 'Every "electure" (electronic lecture) should be designed to include questions for discussion or response among groups of students, rather than simply representing one way transmission of "knowledge" The students, as well as the instructor, should be encouraged to raise new topics and ask questions of the class; and to respond to one another's contributions' which the Learning Platform was able to do. On the empirical data side Liaister and Kobek (2001), go on to highlight that 'Empirical: Research shows that collaborative learning compared to individual and competitive learning scenarios brings students to a higher achievement level, raises their problem solving- abilities, offers cognitive advantages to learners and also has positive influences in enhancing the development of personality traits that are beneficial for future learning'. Students that need to be fully monitored are 'those who have difficulties in interacting in groups in general in case they do not take part in the benefits of these collaborative processes (Laister et al, 2001).

The curriculum project employed elements which where synchronous and asynchrous (Preece 2000). As the delivery method was face to face in a small group setting and online. This blended approach was used with the following key features, curriculum pathways focused on numeracy and literacy. The course on average was for 30 hours of work and included audio, video, online tests and assignment work. In addition e-Learning course resources were available on the LP 24/7. Personalised blogs and collaborative journals for students to access 24/7 were created and assessment was by online submission of assignments and tasks. Examples of the course materials developed by the Keyworker are shown below in the form of screen shots taken directly from the VLE:

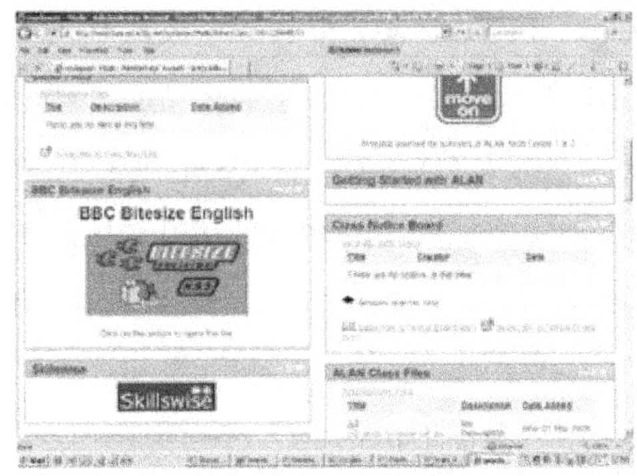

Screen shot 1 : Literacy pathway resources

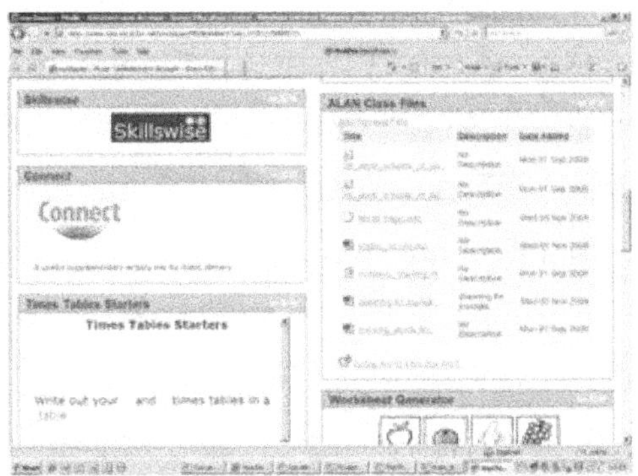

Screen shot 2: Numeracy pathway screenshots

In practice the project goal was curriculum attainment in literacy and numeracy in the form of ALAN level 1 and 2 exams. The co-hort where interviewed with parents and curriculum goals explained in detail and personalised programme set up once diagnostics assessments occurred. This was to further personal understanding and Solomon and Rogers (2001), also highlight the need for short term academic goals for personal success and self efficacy. It is thus key that young people understand the relevance and for this a partnership approach between the school, parents, mentors and Key workers will occur. In addition McCombs and Whisler (1989), confirm that intrinsic motivation is higher when learners are completing tasks that they want to do. Furthermore Ryan and Deci (2000) identified that intrinsically motivated learners are more likely to seek out challenges and extrinsically motivated learners are more likely to seek rewards such as grades and social recognition.

4.4.2 ICT Training for Keyworker

Part of the funding was set aside to employ and train a e-Learning Key worker who would work fulltime with the students in small groups. ICT training was a key part of the project and Appendix 2 highlights the 'Training Design Factors Key Questions Form' (PRU 2010) which was used to identify the personalised training needs of the Key worker. This was based around peer observation and in-house training and as Richards et al, (2009:1) cite that peer observation *".. Is often recommended as a means of improving teacher effectiveness of promoting staff development"*. Table 4.4.2.1 is the Action Plan which was implemented.

Expected Outcomes	Success Criteria	Method of analysis	Timescale
• Creation of online VLE training classroom	Training virtual classroom created – Peer Mentor assigned	Completion of training tasks	September – Novembers 2009
• e-Learning Keyworker using VLE	Monthly training sessions with County User Group and Peer Mentor	Completion of training program and engagement with presentations/ workshops	April 2010
• Student virtual learning classrooms set up by Keyworker	Literacy and Numeracy resources accessed by students	Students attendance and engagement – questionnaire analysis	April 2011
• Increase in students attainment for school	Increase in cohort students attainment in Level 1 Literacy and Numeracy	Analysis of academic attainment results	July 2011

Table 4.4.2.1 - Action Plan to identify training opportunities for Keyworker

4.5   Data Collection

There are several stages for the planning of a survey including piloting the survey as Cohen et al, (2003) identify a *'a rigorous survey formulates clear, specific objectives and research questions'*. This was conducted and two students took part in this process. The School based key worker and Connexions worker also contributed feedback to gauge perceptions on motivation for robust triangulation, which will be discussed later on in this chapter.

There are several forms of questionnaire surveys which might be employed; longitudinal, cross-sectional and prediction surveys (Cohen et al, 2011). In addition sampling error is reduced as the study remains with the same sample over time but a word of caution it may be time consuming (Cohen et al, 2003). Longitudinal studies have the advantage of establishing reliable inferences and establishing causal relationships and this retrospective longitudinal study will focus on the cohort that have reached the end of the project after the 6 weeks. The strength of a cohort analysis is defined by Cohen et al, (2003:176) as almost catching the *'changing properties of individuals'*.

4.5.1 Questionnaires

Questionnaire surveys will provide the main vehicle to gather the opinions and experiences. There are several types of descriptive survey which may be carried out in different settings (Cohen et al, 2003). The include being exploratory where there are no clear models or theories to be tested or in this case confirmatory as this research study hypothesis that ICT can increase student motivation (Cohen et al, 2011).

Creswell (2003), explains further, questionnaires allow the researcher to collect a large volume of information on a limited budget and in a short time.

Furthermore the questionnaire survey will enable a comparative analysis to be carried out, which will allow relationships and connections to be identified. The personal data which was collected through the questionnaire will be kept confidential and the school, students and parents where assured of this. Cohen et al (2011), identify a staged sequence when planning and designing a questionnaire, with objectives at the start, population characteristics, and deciding on how the relevant data can be gathered.

In addition Bell (2005), highlights the advantage that questionnaires are easily analysed interpreted. The analysis for the questionnaire for this study has been broken down question by question and graphically represented. Key findings are stated at the start. Furthermore respondents where giving privacy to fill in the questionnaires (Burton et al, 2008) and this provided much clearer objective results (Cohen et al, 2011). Furthermore the questionnaires will be administered and gathered in person by Keyworker as questionnaires traditionally have a poor response rate (Cohen et al, 2007). Students will be given forty minutes to complete them. The main disadvantage of this mode of delivery is that respondents may feel pressurised to complete the questionnaire within a time limit, and may feel uncomfortable recording sensitive or negative comments (Cohen et al, 2007).

4.5.2 Questionnaire Design

Questions on motivation used elements from the Patterns of Adaptive Learning Survey (PALS) used by Passey et al (2004). Highly structured and closed questions where chosen as the frequencies of responses on the Likert Scale will be able to be statistically analysed and patterns identified. Dichotomous questions which needed a yes / no answer was favoured as it completed the respondent to come off the fence, a point made by Cohen et al (2003). Factors in questionnaire design such as loaded questions, highbrow and complex questions where avoided due to the age of the co-hort (Cohen et al, 2003). In addition the authors highlight the appearance of the

questionnaire as important. The questionnaire font was large and spread
across one side of A4. The purpose of the questionnaire was stated at the
start again good practice identified by Cohen et al, (2011). Emboldening to
draw the respondents attention was another technique employed as
suggested by Cohen et al, (2011).

4.5.3 Likert Scale

The questionnaire was designed with a five point Likert type scale. Likert
(1932) developed this tool of measuring attitudes by asking people to respond
to a series of statements to the extent to which they agree with them, and so
tapping into the cognitive and affective components of attitudes. In addition a
Likert-type scale assumes that the strength/intensity of experience is linear,
i.e. on a continuum from strongly agree to strongly disagree, and makes the
assumption that attitudes can be measured (Mcleod, 2008). Weaknesses of
this tool include respondents answering what they think they should feel then
how they do feel and a limit of using a scale which may show there bias but
not how strongly they agree or disagree with the use of five point scale
(Kothari, 2004).

4.6   Secondary Data Collection

As Creswell (2003) states, secondary data depends on the previously
published academic studies and theories. The process of gathering the
evidence had to depend on this triangulation for an informed rather than
intuitive judgement on the research question. Further   discussion of the case
study triangulation will occur later on in this chapter and will lead onto the data
analysis procedures and the limitations of the research. Secondary data is
primarily collected through desk-based research. According to Jackson (1994)
the value of a research is related to its data collection methods and

importantly, whether or not it includes both secondary and primary data. Furthermore Creswell (2003) states, secondary data, which is an unobtrusive data collection method, depends on the location of pertinent and verifiable previously published academic studies and theories. After locating such data, the researcher should critically evaluate it in order to make sure that it is valid and reliable. This means that the researcher should only include in his study secondary data which is presented in academic researchers and articles which are verifiable and well-referenced (Creswell, 2003). Out of this consideration, the researcher of this study only used data which was obtained from electronic databases or libraries, articles or books and which was scholarly.

4.7   Types of Interviews

Burton et al, (2008) suggest that interviews are useful for obtaining sensitive in-depth information and the importance to identified key respondents to provide answers to the research questions. Disadvantages highlighted include low response rate and lack of context (Burton et al, 2008 and Cohen et al 2011). This will be avoided as only key staffs that have worked with the student identified will take part in this process.

Standardised open ended interviews, with exact wording and sequence of questions where chosen in advance. The questions focused on staff perceptions of ICT and motivational levels of students. The Key worker and Connexions PA where given the same questions. This approach Cohen et al (2003), suggests facilitates the organisation and analysis of the data. Disadvantages again include respondents feeling constrained and limiting naturalness.

One final semi-structured interview will be carried out with the Head Teacher of the PRU (Appendix 3) who has overall responsibility for all intervention curriculum projects across the LA. The interview will examine the strategic vision of the project and how the LA's Upper Schools could best implement this to lead whole school improvement. The Head teachers interview was an interview guide approach as benefits included the interview remained situational (Cohen et al, 2003). This semi-structured interview also had open ended questions to invite an honest and personal comment as Cohen et al (2003) discuss. In addition it puts the responsibility into the respondent's hand, which should allow more ownership (Cohen et al, 2003).

The Upper School did not want to have audio recordings of the interviews and this decision was respected. Audio-recording would have been a relatively unobtrusive method of keeping a permanent record of an interview, which can be inspected by other researchers to ensure validity (Denscombe 2007). The PRU Head teacher agreed to audio interview. Audiotapes should be collected to study the talk of a session or of an ethnographic interview (Spradley, 1979), and in this case technology was used and an audio software captured the interview with the Head teacher.

4.8   Thematic Analysis

The e-Learning Keyworkers and Connexions Worker will be invited to complete the interview questions which can be seen in Appendix 4. The common theme will be to gauge their perception of whether students increased their motivation by this ICT focused approach and the Head teachers interview will also be used for this purpose. All the data across the interviews and audio interview will then be evaluated and as Aronson (1994:1) states *"when gathering sub-themes to obtain a comprehensive view of the information, it is easy to see a pattern emerging"*, in our case student motivation. This approach is favoured as it is a way to analyse in themes about their people's experiences (Mahrer, 1988; Spradley, 1979; Taylor & Bogdan, 1984).

4.8.1   Statistical Analysis

The initial stage for the statistical analysis will be to evaluate the schools attainment in relation to the LA. Student attainment will be looked and percentage pass rate identified by year group in Literacy and Numeracy. Excel will be used as a tool for this. Student attendance percentage will also be worked out by counting the number of sessions should have entered to the number they actually entered and converting this to a percentage. This will then be compared to school trends and the schools target percentage.

The questionnaire survey data type gathered is part ordinal and will include the median value, and the frequencies to the response of the student questionnaires. Key areas of focus will be, do the results tend to cluster around one or two categories of the Likert scale and PALS motivational criteria (Passey et al, 2004). What will be closely looked are the scores and if they cluster around the mean and what the trends are showing. The selection of the sample will be non-probability sampling as a particular group will be targeted. It is a method of purposive sampling and as Cohen et al (2011) highlight built to the specific needs of the project.

4.9   Research Ethics

Educational research must have a moral base which needs to be applied. In line with the BERA (2012) guidelines, the best interests and rights of the child should be the primary consideration when conducting research with children and/or young people. There is a duty to ensure the method is appropriate and will not cause participants any physical or psychological harm (Alderson & Morrow, 2011). In addition active consent was undertaken as all parents and students signed an agreement at the start of the project, which follows BERA (2004) guidelines for research involving young people. The ethics protocol will be agreed in advance of the main study. Burton et al (2008,) state some of the ethical issues that have been considered i.e. anonymity, protection against harmful consequences, protection of privacy and finally giving voice and ownership to participants

Furthermore Burton and Bartlett (2005), highlighted a further issue of ethics which is the need to explain to the respondents the issues of anonymity and confidentiality and access to the findings. This also occurred and the process was carried out by the key staff involved in the project. In addition students and parents will be told during the interview process of this and will have access to the conclusions of the research report. Furthermore Hayes (2006), urges to take note of the following guidelines for a case study i.e. honesty and openness are essential to retain the trust of respondents (with due attention to confidentiality) and as publication of results might expose individuals or institutions it is vital to build in safeguards such as pseudonyms, anonymity and 'a right of reply' from key subjects of the study. Much of these issues will be discussed with students and their parents during the initial interview process.

4.10   Limitations

Every study has a set of limitations (Leedy et al, 2005), or "*potential weaknesses or problems with the study identified by the researcher"* (Creswell, 2005:198). As described in greater detail below, internal validity refers to the likelihood that the results of the study actually mean what the researcher indicates they mean. Explicitly stating the research limitations is vital in order to allow other researchers to replicate the study or expand on a study (Creswell, 2005). Additionally, by explicitly stating the limitations of the research, a researcher can help other researchers "*judge to what extent the findings can or cannot be generalized to other people and situations"* (Creswell, 2005: 198). Limitations of this research include the students were all volunteers who may have withdrawn from the study at any time and the co-hort was relatively small with twenty pupils identified at the start of the project and fifteen at the end. Generalising the impact of the project to a wider student may become an issue. The participants who finish the study might not, therefore, be truly representative of the population (Cohen et al, 2003).

4.11 Establishing Reliability and Validity

Every study must address threats to validity and reliability (Leedy & Ormrod, 2005: 31) *"the validity and reliability of your measurement instruments influences the extent to which you can learn something about the phenomenon you are studying…and the extent to which you can draw meaningful conclusions from your data")*. In practice reliability can be established in four different ways: equivalency, stability, and internal consistency (Carmines et al, 1991).

Carmines et al (1991), define the criteria of internal consistency with comparing the results of using an instrument or process with some external standard which this process met. In this study as a questionnaire was used and internal consistency occurred as there was a strong correlation of the Likert attitudes of the respondent responses to the questions as well as increase in attainment by looking at the percentage breakdown of results in national exams in Literacy and Numeracy. This research also looked to the work conducted on motivational impact of ICT by Passey et al (2005) and the set of motivational indicators used for further triangulation which is discussed in more detail later on in this chapter.

Validity refers to a researchers' ability to *"draw meaningful and justifiable inferences from scores about a sample or population"* (Creswell, 2005: 600). Validity of an instrument refers to *"the extent to which the instrument measures what it is supposed to measure"* (Leedy et al, 2005: 31). In terms of the design of the study does the questionnaire do what it is supposed to measure and does it comply with validity issues? The questionnaire was based around the PALS motivational indicators (Passey et al, 2005) and as thus it measured motivational impacts meeting the requirement for face validity (Cohen et al, 2007). The two most common validity issues are internal validity and external validity. To focus on internal validity the authors refer to the *"extent to which its design and the data that it yields allow the researcher to draw accurate conclusions about cause-and-effect and other relationships within the data"* (Leedy et al, 2005: 103-4). The external validity is validated on the extensive research study undertaken on how ICT is a motivational tool for young learners (Passey et al, 2004).

In survey-based research, the term content validity refers to the degree to which items in an instrument reflect the generalised view, and the statistical conclusion validity refers to the assessment of the mathematical relationships between variables (Leedy et al, 2005).

4.12   Triangulation

Triangulation, used in all types of qualitative research refers to the process of using multiple data collection methods, data sources, analysis, or theories to check the validity of the findings (Leedy et al, 2005) and in fact to add rigor, breadth, and depth to any investigation. This research study uses the findings of national studies into the motivational impact of ICT (Passey et al, 2005), student questionnaires and thematic analysis of interviews and questions with the co-hort Keyworkers, Connexions PA and the PRU Headteacher. This is also backed up by the statistical analysis of students attainment in national exams in Literacy and Numeracy as well as the percentage attendance breakdown. This process should ensure a more convincing and accurate conclusion and set of recommendations.

4.13   Summary

As human motivation theories are complex and many models exist purely having a positivistic approach is less likely to be successful (Cohen et al, 2011). An interpretive approach leans towards inductive-deductive reasoning. This research study leans towards the deductive approach but is dynamic enough to allow the process of observation to hypothesis to oscillate. It is the combination of all of these processes which will allow the development and testing of hypotheses, and then refinement leading into the creation of a conceptual framework (Cohen et al, 2011).

Chapter 5: Presentation of Results

5.1   Introduction

The aim for this section will be present the results of data collected from the
questionnaire survey structured around the Likert Scale. In addition a thematic
overview of the motivational impact of the use of ICT from key staff involved
will be summarised.

Finally a breakdown of attainment and attendance of students involved with
the project will be presented using EXCEL.

5.2   Results of the Student Questionnaire

The questionnaire for the students used a five point Likert type scale. The
results are shown below in Table 5.2.1 and are based on the 15 participants
which took part in the survey (Appendix 5).

Question No.	Strongly Disagree	Somewhat Disagree	Neutral	Somewhat Agree	Strongly Agree
1 Is school work using ICT is more interesting?	3	2	0	3	7
2 Do you find all of your school work interesting?	6	7	2	0	0
3 Do you pay more attention in lessons when they involve ICT?	2	3	1	2	7
4 Do you find ICT you to understand things better because you can see and hear content?	2	2	0	2	9
5 Is using ICT better for your future career and needs?	0	1	2	7	5
6 Do you work worked harder when using ICT ie when you have to produce word processed documents instead of writing?	3	1	1	3	7
7 When asked if they liked working harder with ICT because it helps me work better with other people	1	2	1	2	9
8 Do you concentrate for longer when using ICT?	1	2	1	2	9

Table 5.2.1 - Student Motivational questionnaire data tally for each question based on PALS indicators (Passey et al, 2005)

1) For Question 1 when asked if school work with ICT is more interesting
there was consistency of response with 7 students favouring 'strongly agree'.
When taking into account the positive replies of 'agree' and 'strongly agree'
75% of the respondents fall within this category. As such there is perceived
intrinsic motivation in the majority of students to engage with ICT and e-
Learning as a tool.

2) For question 2 when asked if the students found all of their school work
interesting and there is no clear pattern that can be drawn as all of the student
either disagree or strongly disagree. There is no polarisation of results and
outliers present (Cohen et al, 2005). As students are considered to be
disaffected from the normal mainstream curriculum this result was not
surprising.

3) When asked if the students paid more attention in lessons when it involved
ICT (Question 3) the majority of students (7 out of the 15 respondents)
strongly agree. There is some polarisation of results as 4 students did
somewhat disagree.

4) When asked if ICT helps the students to understand things better because
they can see and hear examples in pictures and video for Question 4, the
majority of students strongly agree (60%).

5) When asked if using ICT now, will be better for their future careers and
needs the majority of students results indicate consistency (11 students either
agree or strongly agree) that ICT is important to a future career or
employment thus offering them further future possibilities.

6) When asked if the students worked harder with ICT because it helps with
their writing again the results are across the range with but over 50% of the
students strongly agree (7 students out of 15).

7) For Question 7 when asked if they liked working harder with ICT because it helps them work better with other people, answers where consistent and the majority strongly agree (9 students out of 15 respondents).

8) When asked if they can work longer without losing concentration when using ICT (Question 8) again the same profile where the majority of students strongly agree.

5.3   Results for the Likert Scale

Each students respondents answers where allocated a score based on the Likert scale :

1. = strongly disagree
2. = disagree
3. = undecided
4. = agree
5. = strongly agree

The final score for each question was collated the sum of their ratings shown below for this summated scale is shown below in Table 5.3.1.

Question No.	Strongly Disagree	Somewhat Disagree	Neutral	Somewhat Agree	Strongly Agree
1	15	10	0	15	35
2	30	35	10	0	0
3	10	15	5	10	35
4	15	10	0	10	45
5	0	5	10	35	30
6	15	5	5	15	35
7	5	10	5	10	45
8	5	10	5	10	45

Table 5.3.1 - Summative scale of the raw scores for pupil questionnaire data

The mean was then calculated based on 15 student respondents (Table 5.3.2) and any mean above 2.5 indicates an overall agreement with the baseline set by the PALS questionnaire analysis carried out by Passey et al (2005).

Question No.	Strongly Disagree	Somewhat Disagree	Neutral	Somewhat Agree	Strongly Agree
1	1	0.6	0	1	2.3
2	2	2.3	0.6	0	0
3	0.6	1	0.3	0.6	2.3
4	1	0.6	0	0.6	3
5	0	0.3	0.6	2.3	2
6	1	0.3	0.3	1	2.3
7	0.3	0.6	0.3	0.6	3
8	0.3	0.6	0.3	0.6	3

Table 5.3.2 - Mean calculations for each question

If we analyse the results using Passey et al (2004) PALS motivational profile the following results are shown for our project co-hort in Table 5.3.3.

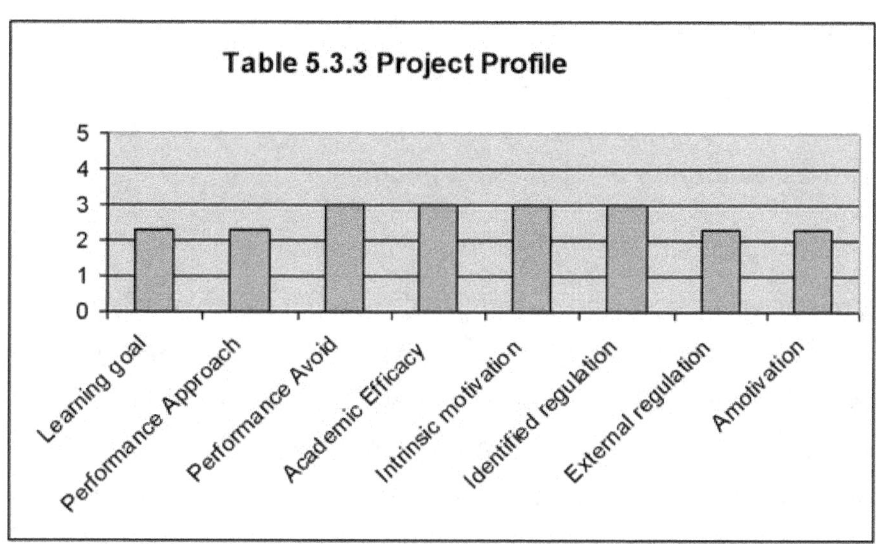

In examining each statement care should be taken to note the 'direction' of the statement as some express negative attitudes i.e. question 2. Table 2 below shows however that the average response is very positive. ICT is enjoyed and seen to make a valuable contribution to school work. By graphically representing student responses using the Likert Scale there is a positive gradient and Figure 5.3.1 clearly shows that students felt that ICT was a motivational tool as the line graph slope is positive towards the 'strongly agree'. This positive slope and correlation demonstrates a positive correlation between the x and y, with the x being the Likert scale. The question which resulted in peaks of strongly disagree where question 2 which was a general question about school work being interesting which can be discarded.

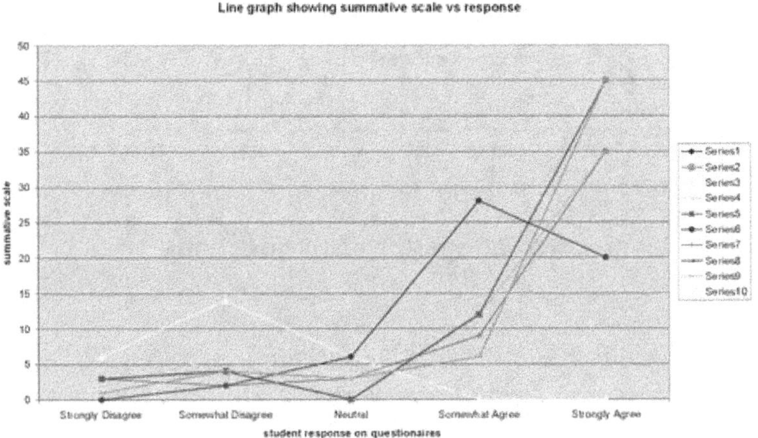

Figure 5.3.1 - Graph representing student responses for questionnaire using 5 point Likert scale

5.4   Thematic Summary of Staff Perceptions

The interviews from the Key worker and Connexions PA where analysed by focusing on the common theme of student motivation. This approach to focus on themes was favoured by a number of thematic analysis researchers (Mahrer, 1988; Spradley, 1979; Taylor & Bogdan, 1984). Comments from the Keyworker questionnaire where *'Student G uses the resources on the Learning Platform out of school and was excited about this opportunity'* and

'Students are motivated to use this and like to see an improvement in results and progress'. Comments from the Connexions PA relating to specific students include *'students are filling their potential and students and parents recognise this as way to get more qualifications'.* To add further validity comments from the Head teacher he stated that there where various strategies to engage young learners including teaching and learning strategies, differentiation and resources delivered by qualified staff. Interestingly he noted that ICT has no benefit purse unless it's delivered by people that know what they are doing.

5.5   Analysis of Student Attainment

The first stage of the evaluation was to breakdown the 2011 achievement data for the Upper School setting the background context. The LA's % 5 A-C* (and equivalent) results was 50% for the project year and the Upper School chosen for the case study had an overall pass rate of 24% (Figure 5.5.1).

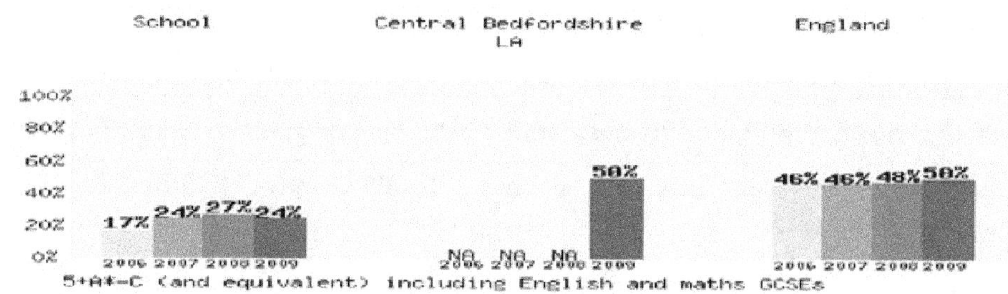

Figure 5.5.1 - Project School 5 A-C % results compared to LA and national average (Source: DCSF 2009).

The project co-hort where entered for Adult Literacy and Numeracy (ALAN) exams which are national accreditations. Adult Literacy and Adult Numeracy qualifications sit under the Skills for Life umbrella often referred to as Adult Basic Skills, they can be taken by learners of any age (Source: EDXCEL

2010) . Learners who attain a Literacy and Numeracy qualification at Level 1/2 will achieve the point's equivalent to half a GCSE in literacy and numeracy. Table 5.5.1 where the results obtained by the student co-hort:

Results Table					
	Year 10	Year 11	Co-hort predicted grades	Overall Project Co-hort Results	Year 11 School results
Literacy level 1	70%	100%	50%	85%	93%
Literacy level 2	10%	20%	0	15%	39%
Numeracy level 1	45%	60%	25%	53%	93%
Numeracy level 2	9%	60%	0	35%	39%

Table 5.5.1 - Literacy and numeracy results for the project co-hort

Evaluation of the attainment was broken down by the percentage of students passing the ALAN Literacy and Numeracy online exams at Level 1 and 2. Quantitative Analysis of ALAN Literacy and Numeracy Exams yielded the following data. Breaking down the percentage it was found that 100% of the Year 11 cohort achieved at least one level 1 qualification (Table 5.5.1 and Figure 5.5.2).

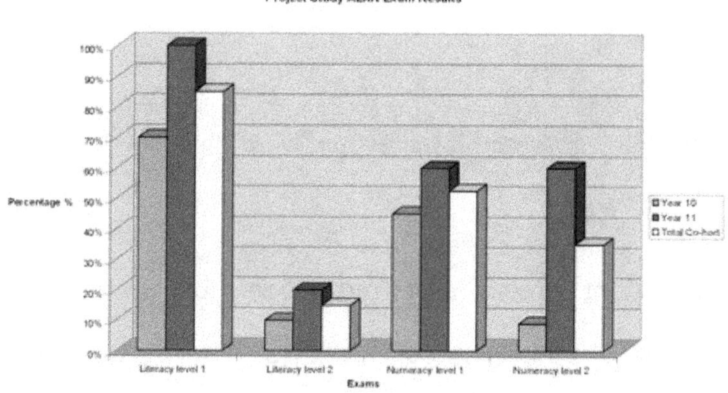

Figure 5.5.2 - Co-hort % exam results in Literacy and Numeracy

5.6   Analysis of Student Attendance

The e-Learning Key worker reported that pupil's attendance noticeably improved whilst on the project. The % attendance was worked out by the number of sessions students where supposed to attend over a six week period to those that where attended. Comparison with the schools percentage attendance shows this was almost inline. Before most students where considered to be Persistent Absentees (PA) by the Keyworker with an average below 70% (Figure 5.6.1).

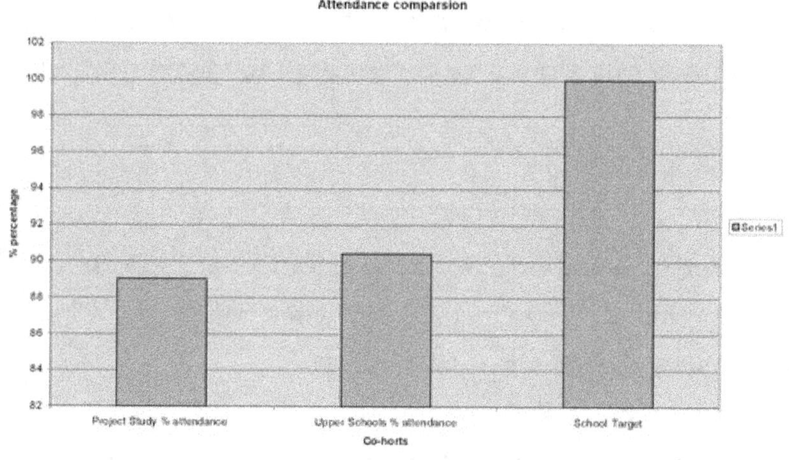

Figure 5.6.1 - Project co-hort % attendance compared to schools and target percentage

Chapter 6:   Evaluation and Discussion of the Results

This chapter aims to discuss the research questions set out for this project study:

- What were the student perceptions on motivational levels when using virtual learning and was this supported by key staff involved with the project?
- What was the impact on student attainment and exam results?
- What was the impact on student's attendance whilst on the project taking into account school trends?

The discussion will be focused around the data collected and will also refer to the literature review.

6.1   Key Question 1:

What were the student perceptions on motivational levels when using virtual learning and was this supported by key staff involved with the project?

The findings of the student questionnaire survey indicate that pupils are generally positive and strongly agree that ICT motivates, makes them learn more effectively and work with others collaboratively.

The majority of the students identified that using ICT to complete school work was more interesting (75%). As such there is an intrinsic motivation in the majority of students to engage with ICT and e-Learning as a tool. In addition

McCombs and Whisler (1989) confirm that intrinsic motivation is higher when learners are completing tasks that they want to do. This is also a learning goal in terms of motivational indicator for classroom practice as defined by Passey et al (2004). Again student perception in terms of concentrating and paying more attention when using ICT in lessons was positive with two thirds of respondents supporting this. ICT uses help pupils to feel that their work is better and therefore that they can succeed to a greater extent. Over half of the students also felt that ICT helped to understand things better because they can see and hear examples in pictures and video. A valid conclusion can be made that students find ICT helpful in understanding as it tapped into learning styles. The Gilbert Report (DfES, 2006) expands on this and presents a vision for personalising teaching and learning using innovative methods such as e-Learning (DfES, 2006).

The use of ICT in a future career was deemed to be important by 11 of the 15 student respondents. The Centre for Research on the Wider Benefits of Learning (DfES 2006b) found that, as well as influencing the obvious outcomes for example, qualifications and career, learning can positively affect health and well-being, attitudes and behaviour.

Students felt they worked harder with ICT because it helped them with their writing again this is an intrinsic motivational indicator. Furthermore students felt they concentrated and focused more using ICT and as such they will be more inclined to be successful (DfES, 2001).

Headlines on student attainment conclude that 100% of the Year 11 cohort achieved at least one level 1 qualification (Table 2).compared to the schools result of 93% for Year 11 students (Chart 4 shows comparison of project co-hort vs schools). Machin and McNally (2006) found strong evidence that education in childhood improves future opportunities, and as such this result was pleasing.

Only one student was permanently excluded by the end of the project, and most were considered to be at risk of permanent exclusions by pastoral staff, a common feature for disaffected students (Becta, 2007).

The findings of the student questionnaire survey indicate that pupils are generally positive and strongly agree that ICT motivates, makes them learn more effectively and work with others collaboratively. Analysis of the questionnaire demonstrated the positive motivational characteristics as defined by Passey et al (2004), when students focused on working with ICT, by relatively high levels of learning and performance approach goals.

The majority of the students identified that using ICT to complete school work was more interesting (75%). As such there is an intrinsic motivation in the majority of students to engage with ICT and e-Learning as a tool. Again this is also a learning goal in terms of motivational indicator for classroom practice as defined by Passey et al (2004). In addition student perception in terms of concentrating and paying more attention when using ICT in lessons was positive with two thirds of respondents supporting this. Analysis of the mean of 3, which was above the 2.5 baseline set by Passey et al (2005) making this a significant result in terms of a motivational indicator. The results also indicate that the use of ICT help pupils to feel that their work is better and therefore that they can succeed to a greater extent. Over half of the students also felt that ICT helped to understand things better because they can see and hear examples in pictures and video. A valid conclusion can be made that students find ICT helpful in understanding as it tapped into learning styles by the use of synchrous and asynchronous resources (Preece, 2000). Students where also encouraged to use their phones and other mobile technologies in lessons. Furthermore Ryan and Deci (2000) identified that intrinsically motivated learners are more likely to seek out challenges.

Students felt they worked harder with ICT because it helped them with their writing again this is an intrinsic motivational indicator (Passey et al, 2004). Furthermore students felt they concentrated and focused more using ICT and as such they will be more inclined to be successful. In addition pupils also felt that ICT was important for their future goals. Analysis of the mean of 3, which was above the 2.5 baseline set by Passey et al (2005) making this a significant result in terms of a motivational indicator.

To support student perception we need to take into account the key staff involved with the project. This includes the e-Learning Keyworker, Connexions PA and Head teacher of the PRU. Comments from the Key worker awhere *Student G uses the resources on the Learning Platform out of school and was excited about this opportunity'* and *'Students are motivated to use this and like to see an improvement in results and progress'*. Comments from the Connexions PA Advisor relating to specific students include *'students are filling their potential and students and parents recognise this as way to get more qualifications'*. To add further validity to the thematic analysis the PRU Head teacher interview views where incorporated. The Head teacher of the PRU is an experienced professional that has worked at the PRU for over ten years. In his interview he stated various strategies to engage young learners noted that ICT has no benefit purse unless it's delivered by people that know what they are doing, personalising learning resources, using peer mentors and partnership approach with families.

6.2   Key Question 2:

What was the impact on student attainment and exam results?

Headlines on student attainment conclude that 100% of the Year 11 cohort achieved at least one level 1 qualification (Table 2).compared to the schools result of 93% for Year 11 students (Chart 4 shows comparison of project co-hort vs. schools). Only one student was permanently excluded by the end of the project, and most were considered to be at risk of permanent exclusions by pastoral staff. All students remained on the project. There were no significance difference in attainment between boys and girls and there was only one girl in the co-hort. If we look at published data from the Department

of Enterprise, Trade and Investment 2006 (from the Office of National
Statistics and DfES releases) nationally 25, 000 achieve no qualifications.
These students where in highlighted as students that may leave with little or
no qualifications under Solomon and Rogers (2005) criteria for disaffection.

6.3   Key Question 3:

**What was the impact on student's attendance whilst on the project
taking into account school trends?**

Teachers and pupils also reported that the motivational impact of ICT
positively affected school attendance. Many of these students where
Persistent Absentees (PA) with an average attendance of 75% at the start of
the program. The project co-horts average by the end of the course was 89%,
only 1% below the schools average. The results showed an improvement in
student's attendance. Furthermore research studies such as Passey et al
(2005:34) conclude *'ICT had supported attendance of pupils who did not
attend schools regularly'*.

6.4   Key Findings Summary

Analysis of the questionnaire demonstrated positive motivational characteristics as defined by Passey et al (2004), when students focused on working with ICT, by relatively high levels of learning and performance approach goals. The use of ICT was focussed on the process of learning and this became a motivational tool which young learners engaged and the e-Learning Key worker reported that students where motivated to use ICT word-processing packages to improve the quality of their work and take pride in the way it was presented.

The majority of students found using ICT more interesting when doing school work as well as paying more attention students enjoyed using the kinaesthetic side of ICT ie videos, audio files. Two thirds of the   of students (75%) felt they concentrated more when using ICT and the e-Learning Key worker reported that pupils are better behaved in lessons which involved ICT, and this is supported by a drop in incidents reported to the schools behaviour log. Teachers and pupils reported that the motivational impact of ICT positively affected school attendance. Project study co-hort attendance increased and was very near the schools percentage. Many of these students where Persistent Absentees (PA) at the start of the. Finally the strategic vision of the LA is to continue to work with schools in a partnership approach. And the PRU is keen to share expertise in a partnership approach with the LA and Upper Schools.

6.5   Recommendations

Following on from the study it is possible to make recommendations on motivating students to achieve national accreditation in Literacy and Numeracy. These include the use of innovative ICT such as Learning Platforms and virtual learning for students to access personalised online resources. In addition focus more on ICT opportunities to support collaborative opportunities between students. Staff training is key as is working in a partnership approach with all stakeholders. In our study this included senior leaders in the school, parents, Connexions, PRU and LA School Improvement Partners.

6.6   Limitations of the Study

This study was essentially small-scale in nature. Initially 20 students where approached to take part in the project. Only 16 chose to take part with parental support. One student was permanently excluded at the initial stages of the project. The accuracy and statistical analysis would have been improved if the co-hort would have been larger (Cohen et al, 2011). In fact the four students that did not take part could have been given the questionnaire initially and reasons identified for why they did not want to take part. Generalising the results of such a small co-hort to a larger student population may be became an issue, however this in part is mitigated by Passey et al (2005) national research studies into the impact of ICT and motivation. Questionnaires could have been designed to be given out at the start and at the end of the project (Cohen et al, 2011). This would have meant a more qualitative glimpse into the worst experiences at the start and the process of engaging and success measured. On reflection also the questionnaires could have gathered more details of the student's experiences during their school career both negative and positive.

6.7   Further Areas for Study

This research study has identified how innovative ICT such as VLE's are key in raising the motivation of students and hence achievement and attainment of pupils. Further areas of study could include use of VLE's with larger co-horts of students within other schools with similar co-horts of disaffected students and at risk of being permanently excluded. Students asked to keep online virtual diaries of their experiences on a day to day basis Progress thus could have been followed during the whole project study period. And finally how the use of personalised pathways through e-Learning could be used as method to deliver national accreditation for students taught in mainstream. Learning styles is another area of possible further study and the role of ICT in providing these opportunities.

Chapter 7:   Conclusion

This research study has shown us that student attainment and achievement can be improved if students are motivated and attendance improved. There is much research nationally which has proved that ICT is a motivational tool which can be used to affect long term change and student self-efficacy (Passey et al, 2004). The initial stage of this research study aimed to establish how the co-hort was identified and reasons for this disaffection providing a focus. The lack of self efficacy and intrinsic motivation was discussed (Huitt, 2001) and strategies to engage students including the use of innovative ICT and virtual learning discussed. The literature review outlined the main findings of using ICT as a motivational tool and this evolved not just only to a discussion of attributes of Learning Platforms and Virtual Learning Environments, but also how the innovative use of these vehicles could lead to opportunities for students (Preece, 2000).

The project student co-hort and the key staff involved provided the vehicle for the quantitative and qualitative data collected. The key staff including the e-Learning Key worker and the Connexions PA and the PRU Head teacher, with the research approach oscillating between the inductive and deductive approach. Analysis of the motivational student questionnaire further supported this research study's conclusion as the Likert scale clearly showed student's perception was that ICT and virtual learning was motivating. Furthermore this motivational change was observed by the Key worker and Connexions PA involved with the project. They were observed to complete tasks which where word-processed and enjoyed using audio and visual ICT resources. These personalised pathway of resources where online on the schools VLE. Attendance of the young learners improved and all of the Year 11 students achieved at least one national qualification in Literacy and Numeracy.

To conclude there is a role for innovative ICT to motivate disaffected learners in virtual classrooms to enhance traditional teaching and learning methods.

Reference List

Alderson, P., & Morrow, V. (2011). *''The Ethics of Research with Children and Young People: A Practical Handbook''*. London: Sage.

Ames, C (1992). *'' Classrooms: Goals, structures, and student motivation''*. *Journal of Educational Psychology*, 84, 261-271.

Aronson, J. (1992). *''The interface of family therapy and a juvenile arbitration and mediation program''*. Unpublished doctoral dissertation, Nova Southeastern University, Fort Lauderdale, FL. http://www.nova.edu/ssss/QR/BackIssues/QR2-1/aronson.html/. Accessed 01/08/2012.

Baguley, T., Banyard, P., Coyne, E., Farrington Flint, L and Selwood, C. (2007) *''Impact 2007: Personalising Learning with Technology''*. Becta.

Bassey, M. (1999). *''Case study research in educational settings''*. Buckingham, Open University Press.

Becta (2006). *''Learning platform functional requirements''*. BECTA . (http://www.maximise-ict.co.uk/LP%20Functional%20Reqs.pdf. Accessed 2/2/2010.

Bedfordshire LA (April 2008): *''Bedfordshire e-Learning vision''* Beds CC. http://www.bedfordshire.gov.uk/Resources/PDF/EducationAndLearning/Governors/GovernorsPDFS/Transforming%20learning%20in%20Bedfordshire%20vi.pdf. (Accessed 2/2/2010.)

British Educational Research Association (2004). *"Revised Ethical Guidelines for Educational Research"*. Cheshire: BERA.

British Educational Research Association (2012). *"The BERA Charter for Research Staff in Education"*. (http://content.yudu.com/Library/A1xl8j/BERACharter/resources/index.htm?ref rerUrl=http%25253A%25252F%25252Ffree.yudu.com%25252Fitem%25252F details%25252F555782%25252FBERA-Charter. Accessed 6/08/2012.

Burton, D. and Bartlett, S. (2005). *"Practitioner Research for Teachers"*. London, Paul Chapman Publishing Ltd.

Burton, N., Brundrett, M. and Jones, M. (2008). *" Research Skills for the Educational Practitioner"*. London: Sage.

Burton, N et al (2008). *" Doing Your Education Research Project"*. Sage: London

BFI. *"Approaches to research"* http://www.bfi.org.uk/filmtvinfo/researchers/approaches_to_research.pdf. (accessed 27/12/2008).

Carr, R. (2011). *"The Theory and Practice of Peer Mentoring in Education Bonus: Free research and peer mentor programs updates"*. Peer Systems Consulting Group, Inc.

Cardno, C. (1998). Working Together: Managing Strategy Collaborating, in Middlewood and Lumby (eds) pp.105-119, *"Strategic Management in Schools and Colleges"*. London, Paul Chapman Publishing Ltd.

Carmines, E., Zellar, R., (1979). *'Reliability and Validity Assessment'*. SAGE.

Condie, R and Munro, B (2007), *"The Impact of ICT in Schools – a Landscape Review"*. Becta.

Cohen, L., Manion, L. and Morrison, K. (2007). *"Research Methods in Education"*. Sixth Edition, Oxon, Routledge.

Cohen, L., Manion, L. & Morrison, K. (2011) *Research methods in education.* 7th ed. London: Routledge.

Creswell, J.W. (2003) *"Research Design: Qualitative, Quantitative and Mixed Method Approaches"*. California: Sage Publications.

Deci, E. L. (1975). *"Intrinsic motivation"* New York: Plenum.

Deci, E., Ryan, R. M. (1985). *"Intrinsic motivation and self-determination in human behaviour"*. New York: Plenum.

Deci, E, Vallerand, R., Ryan, R. (1991). *"Motivation and Education: the Self-Determination Perspective"*., *Educational Psychologist,* 26(3 & 4), 325-346.

DCSF (2007), *"The Children's Plan: Building Brighter Futures"*. HMSO.

DCFS, 2008. *"Formalised peer mentoring pilot evaluation"*. HMSO, London.

Department for Education and Employment (2000). '' *Bulletin Statistics of Education: Survey of Information and Communications Technology in Schools*''. England 2000. London: HMSO

Department for Education and Skills (2001). ''*Bulletin Statistics of Education: Survey of Information and Communications Technology in Schools*''. England 2001. London: HMSO.

DfES (2001a) . ''*NGfL Research and Evaluation Series – ImpaCT 2: Emerging Findings from the Evaluation of the Impact of Information and Communications Technologies on Pupil Attainment*''. London: DfES

DfES (2001b).''*NGfL Research and Evaluation Series No. 4 – Using ICT to enhance home-school links: An evaluation of current practice in* England''. DfES. London.

DfES (2003). ''*Fulfilling the Potential: Transforming teaching and learning through ICT in schools*''. London. DfES.

DfES (2006). ''*The Gilbert report: 2020 Vision: Report of the Teaching and Learning in 2020*''. Review Group. London. DfES.

DfES (2005). '' *Harnessing Technology*''. London. DfES.

DFEE (1998).' '*BUSINESS AND COMMUNITY MENTORING IN SCHOOLS.* London, DFEE.

DfES (2005b), *'The DfES e-Strategy; Harnessing Technology; Transforming Learning and Children's Services'*. HMSO. London.

DfES (2006a). *''Social Mobility: Narrowing Social Class Educational Attainment Gaps''*.
[http://www.dfes.gov.uk/rsgateway/DB/STA/t000657/index.shtml]. Accessed 01.05.2010.

DfES (2006b*), 'The Wider Benefits of Learning: A Synthesis of Findings from the Centre for Research on the Wider Benefits of Learning 1999-2006'*. London, HMSO.

BECTA, (2010).*''NGfL Raising Boys Achievement''*. DCFS: London, HMSO.

Elliott A,. Pekrun R. (2007). *''Emotion in the Hierarchical Model of Approach-Avoidance Achievement Motivation''*. in Schutz, & Pekrun (Eds.), *Emotion in Education* (pp. 57-73). San Diego, CA: Academic Press.

EDXCEL
http://www.edexcel.com/migrationdocuments/Adult%20Literacy%20and%20Adult%20Numeracy/ALAN%20brochure%20for%20web%2030-4-09_A4.pdf.
Accessed 2/02/2011

Fisher Family Trust : http://www.fischertrust.org/dap_overview.aspx. A
Accessed 2/02/2011

Galloway, W., Bpland, S., Benesova, A., (2002) *''Virtual Learning Environments''*. Available at
http://www.dcs.napier.ac.uk/~mm/socbytes/feb2002_i/3.html (accessed on 11/2/2008).

Glanz, J. (1991). *''Action research' Journal of Staff Development''*. Summer 1999 (Vol. 20, No. 3). Available at http://www.nsdc.org/library/publications/jsd/glanz203.cfm. Accessed on 27/12/2008.

Groundwater-Smith, S. and Mockler, N. (2006). *''Research that Counts: practitioner research and the academy''*. in *Counterpoints on the Quality and Impact* of Educational Research, Special Edition of Review of Australian Research in Education, Number 6.

Harlen, W., Crick, R. (2003) Testing and Motivation for Learning, *Assessment in Education: Principles, Policy & Practice*, 10:2, 169 — 20.7

Hattie, J. (2009). *''Visible Learning''*, London Routledge.

Hayes, D. (2006) *''Case study''*. Available at http://www.edu.plymouth.ac.uk/resined/Case_study/casest.htm (Accessed 20 / 01 / 2009).

Hiltz, S. R. (1998) *''Collaborative-Learning in Asynchronous Learning Networks: Building Learning Communities''*. Invited address at WEB98 Orlando Florida, November 1998. Available on http://web.njit.edu/~hiltz/collaborative_learning_in_asynch.htm (Accessed on 15/10/2008).

Hirom, K. & Mitchell, G. (1999). *"The Effect of Mentoring on the Academic Achievement of Boys"*. Paper presented to BERA Annual Conference, Sussex, September 1999.

Hopkins, B. (2008). *"The Peer Mediation and Mentoring Trainer's Manual"*. Optimus Education.

Huitt, W. (2001*). "Motivation to learn: An overview"*. Educational Psychology Interactive. Valdosta, GA: Valdosta State University. Available , from http://chiron.valdosta.edu/whuitt/col/motivation/motivate.html (accessed on 23/12/2008)

HM Government (2007) *" Transformational Government Enabled by Technology"*. London. HMSO.

Johnson, B. & Christensen, L. B. (2012) *Educational research: quantitative, qualitative and mixed approaches.* 4th ed. Thousand Oaks, Calif.: SAGE.

Johnson, J and Dyer, J (2005), *"User-Defined Content in a Constructivist Learning Environment'*:

Joseph Rowntree Foundation (2007). *"Experiences of Poverty and Educational Disadvantag'e'* . Available at [http://www.jrf.org.uk/knowledge/findings/socialpolicy/2123.asp]. Accessed 02/12/2011.

Kaplan, S., (2006) *"Blended Learning Communities"*. Available at EDXCEL http://www.icohere.com/CollaborativeLearning.htm (accessed on 24/12/2008).

Kelly, S. (2006) *"The CPD Co-ordinators Toolkit'.* Paul Chapman Publishing.

Kelly, S., Machell, J., Mchugh, G., and Rogers., C. (2004). *"The Motivational Effect of ICT on Pupils"*. Department of Educational Research Lancaster University.

Kerlinger, F., (1970) *"Foundations of Behavioural Research"*. New York: Holt, Rinehart and Wilson

Kerry, T. and Shelton Mayes, A. (eds) (1995). *"Issues in Mentoring"*. Routledge.

Kibbee, K., Gerzon, J. (2008*). "The MIT Training Guide: Key Questions"*. Massachusetts University.

Kitchen, S. et al. (2007). *"Harnessing Technology Schools Survey 2007"*. Becta. Available at [http://partners.becta.org.uk/index.php?section=rh&catcode=_re_rp_02&rid=1 4110]. Accessed 01/08/2011.

Laister, J.; Koubek, A. (2001)' *"3rd Generation Learning Platforms. Requirements and Motivation for Collaborative-Learning"*. EURODL – European Journal of Open and Distance-Learning, Dec. 2001. Available at http://www.eurodl.org/materials/contrib/2001/icl01/laister.htm (accessed on 23/12/2008.)

Laister, J., Kober, S. (2002). ''*Social Aspects of Collaborative-Learning in Virtual Learning Environments*''. Available at http://comma.doc.ic.ac.uk/inverse/papers/patras/19.pdf (Accessed on 22/11/2008).

Leedy, P. D. Ormrod, J. E. (2005). *''Practical research: Planning and Design''* (8th ed.). Upper Saddle River, NJ: Prentice Hall.

Likert, Rensis (1932). "*A Technique for the Measurement of Attitudes*". Archives of Psychology 140: 1–55.

Machin, S,. McNally, S (2006), *''Education and Child Poverty: Literature Review''*: Joseph Rowntree Foundation. Available at [http://www.jrf.org.uk/bookshop/eBooks/9781859354773.pdf]. Accessed on 01/05/2011.

Mahrer, A. R. (1988). ''Discovery-oriented psychotherapy researc''h. *American Psychologist, 43*(9), 694-702.

Marcoulides, G. A. (1998). *''Modern Methods for Business Research''*. NY: Lawrence Erlbaum Associates.

Maslow, A. (1987). '' *Motivation and Personality''. (3rd Edition)* Harper Collins: New York.

McCombs, B L., Whisler, J S. (1989) "The *Role of Affective Variables in Autonomous Learning*", Educational Psychologist, 24: 3, 277 — 306.

MANDBF, (2010). *"Peer Mentoring in schools'.'* Available at http://www.mandbf.org/wpcontent/uploads/2011/03/Peer_Mentoring_in_Scho ols1.pdf . Accessed 02/11/2011.

McLeod, S. A. (2008). "Simply Psychology; Likert Scale". Accessed 12 April 2012, from http://www.simplypsychology.org/likert-scale.html

Morrison, I., Everton, T. & Rudduck, J. (2000). *" Pupils helping other pupils with their learning: cross-age tutoring in a primary and secondary school".* *Mentoring & Tutoring*, 8, pp. 187-200

National Literacy Trust (2005), *"Every Which Way We Can – a Literacy and Social Inclusion Position Paper":* National Literacy Trust. Available at [http://www.literacytrust.org.uk/socialinclusion/policychallenge.html].Accessed 02-12-201.

Passey, D., Machell, J., Mchugh, G., and Rogers., C. (2004).' *"The Motivational Effect of ICT on Pupils'".* Department of Educational Research Lancaster University.

Passey, D., Williams, S. and Rogers., C (2008). " *Research report Assessing the potential of e-Learning to support re-engagement amongst young people with Not in education, employment or training (NEET) status"* 'BECTA Overview Report 2008.

Preece, J. (2007). '' *Online Communities. Designing, Usability, Supporting Sociability*''. New York, 2000.

Ofsted (1996), *"Exclusion from Secondary Schools 1995/6"*: HMSO.

Ofsted (2009). '' Virtual learning environments: an evaluation of their development in a sample of educational settings''. HMSO.

QCA/NAACE (2007) '' *e-Learning*'', London, 2007.

Reid, K. (2002). '*'Mentoring with disaffected pupils: Mentoring and Tutoring''*. pp. 153-170. London.

Rich, D. (2007),. ''*Parental Involvement in School*''. Available at (www.urbanext.uiuc.edu/succeed/01-parental.html. Accessed on 21/12/ 2007

Russell, G. (2001). ''*Virtual Schools and Educational Futures*''. In Educational Technology (November - December 2001). In Educational technology Publications Inc, New Jersey.

Selwyn, N. *"Teaching Information Technology to the Computer Shy: a theoretical perspective on a practical problem"*. (1997). Journal of vocational education and training. Vol. 10. No. 3. pp 395-408

Simons,J., Dewitte, S., Lens, W. (2004). ''The *role of different types of instrumentality in motivation, study strategies, and performance: Know why you learn, so you'll know what you learn!"*. British Journal of Educational Psychology (2004), 74, 343–360.

Sims, D. (2002). *"Mentoring Young People: Benefits and Considerations"*. Routledge.

Social Exclusion Task Force (2006). *"Reaching Out: An Action Plan on Social Exclusion'*: Cabinet Office. Available at [http://www.cabinetoffice.gov.uk/social_exclusion_task_force/publications/reaching_out/reaching_out.asp]. Accessed on 21/12/ 2007.

Social Exclusion Task Force (2007). *"Context for Social Exclusion Work"* .[http://www.cabinetoffice.gov.uk/social_exclusion_task_force/context]. Online accessed on 21/12/ 2007.

Social Exclusion Unit (1998). *"Truancy and School Exclusion"*.The Stationery Office. Online accessed on 21/12/ 2007.

Social Exclusion Unit (2004). *"Breaking the Cycle of Social Exclusion"* . Available at [http://archive.cabinetoffice.gov.uk/seu/page6396.html]. Accessed on 21/12/ 2007.

Social Exclusion Unit (2005). *"Inclusion through Innovation'*: Office of the Deputy Prime Minister. Available at [http://archive.cabinetoffice.gov.uk/seu/publicationse70c.html?did=768]. Accessed on 21/12/ 2000.

Soller, A. (2001). ''*Supporting Social Interaction in an Intelligent Collaborative-Learning System*'' .' Int. Journal of Artificial Intelligence in Education. 12, 40-62.

Sotto, E. (1994). ''*When Teaching Becomes Learning: a theory and practice of teaching and learning*''. New York: Cassell.

Spradley, J. (1979). ''*The ethnographic interview*''. New York: Holt, Rinehart and Winston.

Stader, D. and Gagnepain, F. G. (2000). ''*Mentoring: The power of peers*'', American Secondary Education, 28 (3), 28-32.

Sukhnandan, L., Lee, B. & Kelleher, S. (2000). ''*An Investigation into Gender Differences and Achievement: phase 2: school and classroom strategies*''., Slough: NFER.

Taylor, S. J., & Bogdan, R. (1984). ''*Introduction to qualitative research methods: The search for meanings*''. New York: John Wiley & Sons.

Trochim, W.M. (2001). ''*The Research Methods Knowledge Base, (2nd ed.)*''. Cincinnati: Atomic Dog Publishing.

Vygotsky, L. S. (1978). ''*Mind in Society*''. Cambridge.

Webb, N. (1984.) *"Microcomputer Learning in Small Groups: Cognitive Requirements and Group Processes"*. Journal of Educational Psychology 1984, Vol. 76(6).

Zull, J. (2002). *"The Art of Changing the Brain: enriching the practice of teaching by exploring the biology of learning"*. Sterling VA: Stylus Publishing.

Appendix 1 Becta Learning Platform Requirements

Table 3.3.1 - Content management

O = obligation M = mandatory R = optional but recommended

Requirement name	O	Description	Notes
R10: Assessment items	M	Assessment items shall be loaded and used.	Platforms shall be able to deal with assessment items including those meeting selected open specifications that define question types and how they can be delivered.
R11: Launch resources	M	The user shall be able to launch digital content via a web browser or other application.	Specified World Wide Web Consortium (W3C) specifications shall be supported, including being able to use the hypertext transfer protocol (http) and the hypertext markup language (html). The appropriate e-Government Interoperability Framework requirements shall be met. Filtering systems that block the receipt of inappropriate materials and access to undesirable websites should be enabled but this is largely the responsibility of the ISP.
R12: Load content objects	M	It shall be possible to load, store and make sharable content objects available to users. Run-time interactions with content objects should be supported. This includes being able to load bundled resources (content packages) and unpack them.	Parts of the SCORM specification shall need to be supported.
R13: Load resources	M	It shall be possible to load digital content into a storage area that can be presented to learners and accessed via the platform interface.	The appropriate file type requirements in the e-Government Interoperability Framework shall be met.
R14: Metadata creation	M	Users shall be able to classify and tag resources.	If metadata is to be shared a profile of the Curriculum Online format shall be used. It is recognised that in order to keep tagging simple not all elements will be needed. Other metadata schemes may be used. It should be possible for local information to be recorded and used and for metadata to be created socially (for example, folksonomy).

Requirement name	O	Description	Notes
R15: Metadata import and display	M	It shall be possible to load and store metadata records and display information derived from them to the user.	There are various possible metadata formats including Curriculum Online and e-Government Metadata Standards (eGMS). It is recognised that there may be a range of metadata provided and it may not be possible to provide consistent information.
R16: Resource creation	M	Users shall be able to create new resources, integrate them with the platform and export them.	It is important that learner can be engaged with digital tools as well as have access to ready-made content. This could include collaborative resource creation, bookmarking and creation of annotations or ratings.
R17: Coursework	R	Schools should be able to submit pupils' coursework (formally agreed and accredited units of study) to examination bodies in an agreed format.	There is no currently agreed specification although some formats have been produced for specific cases. This is also dependent on other issues such as non-repudiation and security. Consideration should also be given to submission of coursework to colleges or for use in a portfolio.
R18: Cross device	R	Resources should be made available to a range of devices.	There is increasing use of various devices to support learning. These will be determined by the context but could include mobile devices such as PDAs and cell phones.
R10: Identifiers	R	Globally unique identification namespaces should be interpreted and managed.	Identification of resources and individuals should be unambiguous. The platform should support the W3C Uniform Resource Identifier (URI) format and specified coding schemes such as the Unique Pupil Number.
R11: Resource lists	R	Lists of resources should be made available in a shareable format.	Reading lists could be exchanged or shared both within and across schools, and with other users and the community.
R12: Syndicate content	R	Users should be able to combine data-streams and selectively share them with others.	Data could be gathered from personal or class-based web logs, news sites and subject-based blogs, podcasts, vodcasts or newsfeeds and sites and distributed as 'remixes' or 'playlists'.

(Source: Becta, 2006:5)

Table 3.3.2 - Curriculum mapping and planning

O = obligation M = mandatory R = optional but recommended

Requirement name	O	Description	Notes
R13: Accessibility	M	The platform interface shall be accessible to users.	It is the responsibility of a platform provider to ensure accessibility guidelines are followed and that legislation such as the Disability Discrimination Act is adhered to. A detailed set of guidelines for accessibility is not considered to be within the scope of this framework and full Web Accessibility Initiative (WAI) AAA requirements may be too restrictive. Requirements for learners and administrators may vary. It is recognised that the platform provider may not have control over the accessibility of content. However, WAI AA level requirements should be met by platform modules.
R14: Assessment for learning	M	The platform shall enable learners to be provided with assessments and diagnostics to support learning plans.	This should include self-review and peer review.
R15: Customisable interface	M	The user interface shall be capable of being customised to adapt to the learner's preferences.	This should include learner interface preferences and accessibility requirements. The user shall be able to change the screen colours, font and font size.
R16: Lesson planning	M	It shall be possible for teachers to produce and manage lesson plans.	HTML or other open formats should be used. A lesson plan specification could be developed in collaboration with all the major stakeholders and it could then be possible to share plans more widely.
R17: Navigation and search	M	Curriculum information shall be used to search for and to navigate to resources within the platform.	A recognised curriculum format shall be used. In particular specified Curriculum Online structures shall be used. Metadata and Topic Maps offer possible ways to express these structures.
R18: Personalisation	M	Users should be able to personalise their learning experience.	This should include using a learner profile to adjust the resources that are presented. The platform should also allow the learner to select aspects of their own learning journey.

| R19: Sequence resources or activities | M | Users shall be able to create structured units and sequence learning resources or activities. | Users should have the ability to use conditional rules that can change the learning experience depending on behaviour. This should include sequencing controlled by the content, teacher or pupil. |
| R20: Metadata harvesting | R | The platform should be able to retrieve metadata instances from distributed repositories. | The platform should have the functionality to query repositories. The Curriculum Online portal is expected to be one example. |

(Source: Becta, 2006:7)

Table 3.3.3 - Learner engagement and administration

O = obligation M = mandatory R = optional but recommended

Requirement name	O	Description	Notes
R21: Access off site	M	Users shall be able to access the learning platform away from the organisation.	The intention is to enable anytime anywhere access and to include all types of users including teachers, pupils and parents. It is recognised, however, that this depends on access to an appropriate infrastructure and upon the license conditions for some published resources.
R22: Authentication	M	Users shall be uniquely identified and verified.	There should be a consistent approach to authentication; for example, every user may have a unique user name and password linked to individual or group roles and privileges and can easily access other systems. Common systems, including Shibboleth, should be used. Providers should take steps to avoid unauthorised access.
R23: Consistent learner information	M	Learner information shall be consistent throughout the platform	There should be minimal duplication of information and processes should be automated to avoid errors and inconsistencies. A hub integration model could be adopted that allows data to be shared and managed across several systems. Learner information could alternatively only be accessed through a single shared service.
R24: Data protection	M	All stored data shall be secure.	Conformance with current legislation and the requirements of the Data Protection Act for personal data shall be required.
R25: Groups and roles	M	It shall be possible for users be allocated to one or more groups and assigned roles.	Roles and permissions affect how users can interact with the platform. Roles include, for example, administrator, teacher, parent or pupil.
R26: Information access	M	Users with privileges shall be able to access appropriate information.	This could include management information exchanged transparently between systems that may be outside the platform. This could also include support for selective disclosure by electing to share information or resources with other users.
R27: Learner information export	M	It shall be possible for learner information to be exported from the platform.	This shall include support for the provision of statutory information to the DfES or other authorities.
R28: Learner information Import	M	It shall be possible for learner information to be imported to the platform.	This shall include support for transfer of learner records between institutions.

Requirement name	O	Description	Notes
R29: Portfolios	M	Users shall be able to create and maintain portfolios for sharing content and to support personal development.	This kind of functionality is sometimes provided as part of an e-portfolio. But 'e-portfolio' has various definitions and there are several functions that can be provided, possibly via links to a range of web services. Portfolios could include goal setting, identifying interests and learning plans. It is expected that there will be further work to help clarify e-portfolio functionality.
R30: Scheduling	M	Access to resources shall be controllable.	Access may depend upon time constraints or be linked to other events. For example, access to a task may be dependent upon successful completion of another task or only be available for a set time linked to a timetable.
R31: Tracking	M	Facilities shall be provided to track learners' support needs and performance.	This shall include reporting whether a learner has completed a particular resource or could include more complex scores or assessment data. Tracking information should be used to provide feedback to learners.
R32: Usage data	M	Information about individual and group usage of the resources shall be available.	Reports shall be generated that summarise how and when the platform and resources are used.
R33: Attendance	R	Support should be provided for the measurement and reporting of attendance.	For example by providing interfaces to support attendance recording by teachers, or integration with automated attendance or tracking devices.
R34: Self-organisation	R	Users should be able to organise and annotate resources.	This should include categorising and making connections, bookmarking, playlists, adding their own comments, tags and ratings. These could be shared with others.
R35: Timetabling	R	A timetable, or an interface to one, should be supported.	This could be linked to a personalised learning space and scheduling of resources.

(Source: Becta, 2006:9)

Table 3.3.4 - Table 4 Tools and services

O = obligation M = mandatory R = optional but recommended

Requirement name	O	Description	Notes
R36: Discussion forums	M	Users shall be able to take part in discussion forums by posting and reading messages.	Both intranet and internet services could be considered and desktop clients as well as web clients. Forums should be manageable, for example, for a particular group for a set period.
R37: Rights management	M	Functionality shall be provided that supports and recognises licensing conditions.	This may be simply to inform the user of any rights. The ability to tag user created resources with rights information, including Creative Commons licences, shall be possible.
R38: Web services	M	The platform shall be capable of transparently interacting with web services using standard protocols.	This requirement does not at this stage specify particular services, just that there is capability to meet web services protocols when they are required. For example, users could search the Curriculum Online portal from within the platform if this functionality is made available.
R39: Audio-visual conferencing	R	Audio- and video-conferencing should be supported.	This should enable voice or visual communication with peers or teachers, for example using voice over internet protocol (VOIP).
R40: Blog	R	Users should be able to create web logs.	This could include a facility for multimedia entries and integration of an e-portfolio with selective disclosure.
R41: Email	R	One-one and one-many messaging should be facilitated.	Email, or a system that is like email, should be available to users for sending and receiving. This should include sending messages to lists of recipients. Though this is likely to be the responsibility of the ISP, a platform should be able to integrate with email.
R42: Knowledge construction	R	Knowledge construction tools should be available.	These should include collaborative tools, such as Wikis, that allow for the shared editing of content. The tools may be within or outside the platform.
R43: Messaging	R	Users should be able to send messages to individuals and groups of users.	Sending SMS text messages to mobile phones should be supported. The messages could be multimedia as well as text.
R44: Other activities	R	Support for non-teaching activities should be provided.	Tools for managing teaching activities should be flexible and usable for non-teaching activities, created and managed both by teachers and pupils as appropriate. Activities could include sports teams, clubs and societies, community action and student projects.
R45: Resource syndication	R	Syndicated content, such as newsfeeds, should be supported.	This should include output, as well as input, of content.

(Source: Becta, 2006:11)

Appendix 2 Training Design Factors Key Questions Form

Training Design Factors Key Questions Form	
Key Questions	**Comments**
Consider these questions to evaluate and prepare the appropriate training delivery method. In order to fully evaluate and select the best training delivery method, review all questions in each of the Training Factors.	
WHAT DO YOU WANT TO ACCOMPLISH?	
What domain of learning is being targeted: knowledge, skills or attitude/behavior?	Knowledge and skill in the use of a VLE is main outcome
Does this training seek to change a behavior, including the manner in which people's emotions, feelings, and attitudes are brought into play?	Confidence will be measure of success
Will the training teach a skill that requires practice and can be measured?	The use of the VLE and ability to create a virtual classroom resourced with Literacy and Numeracy materials
LEARNING OBJECTIVES FACTOR	
What are the desired outcomes of this training?	Desired outcomes are for e-Learning Keyworker to create a virtual classroom resourced with Literacy and Numeracy level 1 resources for students to

RESOURCES FACTORS	
Instructor	
How many instructors are needed?	2
Will training be needed for instructors?	No
How much time will the instructor or presenter need to prepare to teach this training?	1 day
Is there travel involved for the instructor? Hotel costs? Meals?	No
Space/Location	
Is there existing space? Will it need to be changed in any way?	Classroom available with PC and Internet access
How much space is needed? How many rooms are needed?	1 room
Will learners be in one location only?	Yes
Will participants work in their own space/at their own computers?	Yes
Time	
How many hours is this training?	15 hours
Will the training be taught in segments? (For example, will the training be taught in one-hour segments, once per week, for many weeks?)	First four weeks intensive in house ICT training and peer observation schedule
Cost	
Will space need to be rented?	No
Will handouts, supporting documentation, and instructor materials be produced in-house or at a cost from a vendor?	No
Will existing software or computers be used as is, or will they need to be upgraded or purchased?	Existing
What needs to be measured?	Confidence in using VLE by Keyworker Attainment of students
Has a base line been established for measuring?	Yes; Audit to identify staff development needs and perceived attainment of students

Appendix 3 PRU Head teacher Interview Questions

Head teacher Interview Questions

1) Can you tell me a little about your background and how long have you been Head teacher of the PRU?

2) In your experience what strategies help to engage young learners?

3) What do you perceive the benefits of ICT for disaffected students?

4) What is your vision for ICT and e-Learning across the PRU?

5) How would you enable e-maturity across the LA ?

6) Any other comments

Appendix 4 Key Staff Interview Questions

Keystaff Interviews Questions

Date:

1. What is your role with the students?
2. How often do you meet with the students?
3. Have you received training to use the Virtual Learning Platform
4. How have you found this process to be?
5. Are you able to create resources for the online classroom?
6. Have you created any curriculum resources?
7. Have you set any personalised targets with students?
8. Do you feel students are more motivated when they access resources through the VLE?
9. Do you think students are motivated when using ICT i.e. word processing, audio files etc?
10. Any other comments

Thank you for your time.

Appendix 5 – Student Motivationnel Questionnaire

Dear Student,

Only a very few of the students in XXXX have had the opportunity of using e-Learning this year. More students will use it next year and we want to make sure it gets even better. Your feedback and thoughts are really important to us so please could you help us by filling out this survey and returning it by email. Please put a cross in the answer that best fits! Many thanks.

1. Is school work using ICT is more **interesting**?

Strongly Disagree	Somewhat Disagree	Neutral	Somewhat Agree	Strongly Agree

2. Do you find all of your school work interesting?

Strongly Disagree	Somewhat Disagree	Neutral	Somewhat Agree	Strongly Agree

3. Do you pay more **attention** in lessons when they involve ICT ie word-processing, audio files, video files?

Strongly Disagree	Somewhat Disagree	Neutral	Somewhat Agree	Strongly Agree

4. Do you find ICT you to **understand** things better because you can see and hear content i.e. sound files and video files?

Strongly Disagree	Somewhat Disagree	Neutral	Somewhat Agree	Strongly Agree

5. Is using ICT better for your **future career** and needs?

Strongly Disagree	Somewhat Disagree	Neutral	Somewhat Agree	Strongly Agree

6. Do you **work harder** when using ICT i.e. when you have to produce word processed documents instead of writing?

Strongly Disagree	Somewhat Disagree	Neutral	Somewhat Agree	Strongly Agree

7. When asked if they liked working harder with ICT because it helps me work better with other people

Strongly Disagree	Somewhat Disagree	Neutral	Somewhat Agree	Strongly Agree

8. Do you **concentrate** for longer when using ICT?

Strongly Disagree	Somewhat Disagree	Neutral	Somewhat Agree	Strongly Agree

Thank you for your time.